COPLEY SQUARE

COPLEY SQUARE

HISTORY THROUGH ARCHITECTURE

Leslie Humm Cormier, PhD

THE
History
PRESS

Published by The History Press
Charleston, SC
www.historypress.com

Copyright © 2018 by Leslie Humm Cormier, PhD
All rights reserved

Front cover images, clockwise from top: The Boston Public Library; the Courtyard of the Library; and Trinity Church, reflected in the Hancock Tower, a glass skyscraper. *Photographs by K.F.K. Cormier.*
All images by the author unless otherwise noted.

First published 2018

Manufactured in the United States

ISBN 9781625858405

Library of Congress Control Number: 2018932095

Notice: The information in this book is true and complete to the best of our knowledge. It is offered without guarantee on the part of the author or The History Press. The author and The History Press disclaim all liability in connection with the use of this book.

All rights reserved. No part of this book may be reproduced or transmitted in any form whatsoever without prior written permission from the publisher except in the case of brief quotations embodied in critical articles and reviews.

I wish to dedicate my book to my favorite charity, Save the Children, to thank them for their global efforts for the hungry, the sick, the poor and for all children in crisis. Like so many ideas explored in this book, the concept for this charity began almost a century ago in Britain, expanded this vision in America and is today an international force for good.

CONTENTS

Preface	11
Acknowledgements	13
Introduction. Europe and America:	
** A Century of International Architecture in Boston**	15
Geometry and Nature	
Tracing Historical Precedent	
Saving Significant Places	
Suggestions to the Reader: Sight and Sites	
1. America: From Swamp to City Square	23
The River Before the Square	
Building Early Boston	
Copley in the Colony	
Copley in the Academy	
Art Square to Copley Square	
2. America to Europe: Americans Discover Antiquity	33
The Grand Tour: Boston to London to Paris to Rome to Boston	
Antiquity, Architectural Precedent and the Appropriateness of Form	
L'École des Beaux-Arts in Paris	
An American Critique of the Beaux-Arts Style	
International Ideals in Stone and Glass	

Contents

3. America: An Evolving Environment   **41**
    The Changing Configurations of Copley Square
    Some "Common" Boston Place Names
    Boston Celebrates Itself—Often
    The Constitution and Social Causes Considered

4. America: The Societal Significance of Trinity Church   **49**
    Selected Artists and Thinkers of Trinity Church
    A Public Form within a Public Forum
    Arches in American Architecture

5. America: The Art and Architecture of Trinity Church:
    H.H. Richardson, Architect (circa 1875)   **59**
    The Strong and the Simple
    The Forms of Trinity Church
    Site and Precedent in the Square
    Inside Trinity Church
    A Building Defined by Geometry
    Colored Glass and Venetian Color
    Architecture and Allusions

6. Europe and America: International Designs of Cities   **69**
    Urban Models of Two Millennia
    Paris's Boulevards as Models for the Back Bay
    London's Squares as Models for Copley Square
    Urban Design in American Cities
    Grid, Vista and Beaux-Arts Cities in America
    Urban Squares and Beaux-Arts Architecture
    Urban Parks in American Cities
    Contemplating a Copley Canal

7. America: The National Significance of the
    Boston Public Library   **81**
    A Classical Education for Everyman and Its Expression in
        Architectural Form
    Special Collections and Archives of the Boston Public Library
    Selected American and European Architects, Artists and Designers
        of the Boston Public Library

Contents

8. Europe and America: The Architecture and Art of the Boston Public Library: McKim, Mead & White, Architects (1895) — 89
Architecture as Acropolis
Facing the Square: Façade and Elevation of the Boston Public Library
Inside the Boston Public Library
The Arts in Processional Spaces
A Library, Architectural Precedent and L'École in America
The Courtyard of the Boston Public Library
Finding Florence in Copley Square

9. America: Copley Square and the Concept of Architectural Ensemble — 101
Old South Church (circa 1875)
The Copley Plaza Hotel (1912)
The Johnson Building of the Boston Public Library (1972)
Another Kind of Architectural Ensemble: The Boston Public Library as Inspiration for Other Libraries in America
Arches and Inspiration Renewed

10. America: The Skyscraper and the Square — 113
The Hancock Tower, I.M. Pei and Associates (circa 1975)
Reflection, Color and Shape in Copley Square
Clouds and Symbols
Creating Contemporary Architecture to Complement Historic Copley Square

Conclusion. America and Europe: Finding Form in the Square — 119
Celebrating the Square in the City
Copley Square as Café American

A Glossary of Art and Architectural Terms	125
Notes	129
Bibliography	133
Index	137
About the Author	141

PREFACE

I find cities endlessly fascinating. Boston is an excellent city for understanding architectural history and contemporary urban design because it has imported so many urban models and created new models. It is a city that can best be seen on foot and public transit and so is itself a good model for other cities—forward thinking in design. It always has been so. I am honored to study here and to teach and to write on a city that represents the best of American thinking and design in this book.

Though I have spent my career lecturing on art, architecture and urban design here, I am not a native Bostonian, and so I can both read this city with a complementary viewpoint of one who has chosen this environment and, likewise, stand outside it as an observer, sometimes critically. I have learned so much writing this book about Copley Square in Boston; for example, I am still astounded that so much of this city is but gravel landfill over water. This is perplexing to me—the concept of inventing land, in a country of as much landmass as America, seems contradictory.

I have learned that Copley Square literally is floating. Perhaps there is an image in that: perhaps we should creatively seek, through design, to open a section of the pavement and view the water below Copley Square. Add gondolas? At least metaphorically, we will, in this book, look under the surface views into Boston's urban land and watery design history, as well as at its skyline silhouette.

I've also learned a great deal of respect for earlier architects. As a Modernist, it is important for me to appreciate the long history of design that preceded my preferred period. I have come to appreciate architect Charles Follen McKim, who to me personifies the historical chain of significant American artists of the late nineteenth and early twentieth centuries. Both American and European educated, these architects were equally dedicated to European historical values in architecture and to excellent design of their contemporary American public forms. Through his many significant public buildings, McKim shared his ideals with American cities.

Further, I have learned to be impressed by the founders of the Boston Public Library, whose edifice represents one of the bases of freedom in America: the "free" and public access to the intellectual pursuits of books and reading. Ideas are the greatest protectors of freedom, and books have made this dissemination of knowledge possible over millennia. Thus, the Boston Public Library takes its place in the history of the preservation of human rights, a right you are exercising now—through the right to read freely.

Most significantly, Copley Square is also a lesson learned for me as a twentieth-century exercise in understanding and appreciation of humane, particularly pedestrian, space. It is the human-centered antidote to America's postwar planning (for the automobile), and it stands today in very close temporal and physical proximity to that anti-human era of demolition as urban planning. The pedestrian quality of today's Copley Square represents the return of pedestrian scale, design sanity, humanity and decency to cities.

So Copley Square, for me, as it stands today, is a quiet type of urban triumph—the triumph of important symbolic buildings and the triumph of just sitting under a tree in a city, surrounded by meaningful buildings that engage with European history and American freedom.

ACKNOWLEDGEMENTS

My thanks to the editors of The History Press, Amanda Irle and Edward Mack, for their supportive comments and for including me in their roster of writers. Your care for the continuity of books as the legacy of history is greatly applauded by this author. Thank you to The History Press for your commitment to the long tradition of books.

I thank the Boston Public Library; the Boston Architectural College; Wellesley Free Library; and Special Collections, Senate House Library, University of London.

I would like to acknowledge the memory of my former advisor, architectural historian and theorist Professor William H. Jordy, Henry Ledyard Goddard Professor of Brown University, whose writings on nineteenth- and twentieth-century architecture, including "The Beaux-Arts Renaissance: Charles McKim's Boston Public Library," in his book *American Buildings and Their Architects: Progressive and Academic Ideals at the Turn of the Twentieth Century*, became an inspiration for my book. Special thanks also to Daniel Paul, advisor, and one of great insight, for your thoughts on the Charles River.

Thanks to the Boston Architectural College, an institution that has brought Modernism to the Back Bay in striking urban architecture for a creative community. A wave goes out to all my BAC architecture and design students. Thanks to friends Pam for photos of Central Park and Cathy for reading a manuscript chapter.

Acknowledgements

For visuals in this book, I particularly thank my son, talented photographer and chef. My special appreciation is always to my husband, scientist and thinker, who spoke this semester in London, where Isaac Newton once lectured, while I revisited the squares of Bloomsbury. You are my model for a lifetime of curious travel and endless inquiry and my best friend.

INTRODUCTION
EUROPE AND AMERICA

A Century of International Architecture in Boston

Geometry and Nature

Cities are made of stones and spaces, squares and cubes, lines and vistas and sometimes curves and arches. They are works of concrete and water and pavement and trees. Urban places are compositions of the ideals of abstract geometry and nature—ideal forms living amid noise and pedestrians and bicycles and bus traffic. Our cities are our monuments to what it is to be human.

From uninhabitable estuary to sophisticated urban center, Boston's Copley Square holds a unique place in American architectural and urban history—as well as in the life of the contemporary American city. As urban form, Copley Square hearkens back to the pedestrian street life of eighteenth-century Enlightenment London and, within its wider location in Boston's Back Bay, to nineteenth-century Parisian city planning. As architectural history, it illustrates the consciously re-created European designs of the Italian Renaissance piazza and palazzo, as well as a mélange of European historical urban sites.

Such importation of European style was a conscious re-creation of the sophistication of the Old World here in the New World. Well-traveled American architects, from the eighteenth century's Grand Tour to the nineteenth century's École des Beaux-Arts, recalled in their work earlier British, French and Italian models that they had visited, building Boston

Introduction

A century of style in Copley Square.

in their likeness. Their worldly approach to the city endured into the modern era, as Copley Square opened the historical city to the global aesthetics of the twentieth century via the form of the glass skyscraper of the International Style.

Introduction

To appreciate the complex historical components of this city, and to hold the concept of "one century of significant American architecture" concisely in one's mind, rather than memorizing architectural dates (that can vary from initial competition and design to construction and dedication of the building), it is clearer for us to conceive of this place and time as a special era of its own. Thus, we will consider "Copley Square as the urban creation of one hundred years, the century from 1875 to 1975."

As we stand today in the grassy center of Copley Square, we take in a full century of this progression of European-styled American design, represented by a selection of our country's most talented artists and architects: H.H. Richardson, for the stones of Trinity Church (mid-1870s); Charles McKim, of McKim, Mead & White, for the palace-like Boston Public Library (1890s); and I.M. Pei, for the soaring glass Hancock Tower (mid-1970s). Comparing the scale and stylistic advances from the private residential houses of eighteenth-century Beacon Hill to the public architectural edifices of late nineteenth-century Copley Square demonstrates that this American city was at last poised to take its place socially, economically and aesthetically within the wider world—nationally and internationally.

Anchored by the major architecture of H.H. Richardson and Charles Follen McKim, Copley Square has remained vibrantly alive for more than a century. The growing international artistic and architectural sophistication of the city of Boston was affirmed by the worldly work of the French-educated and British-influenced American architects of the late nineteenth century. The new Beaux-Arts architecture of McKim, Mead & White's Boston Public Library, designed with flair and confidence by this widely respected New York firm, set a national American standard for important civic architecture to come.

The eras of these nineteenth- and twentieth-century building programs corresponded with national periods of looking forward, as well as backward. The first coincided with the celebration of the American Centennial of the Declaration of Independence in 1876; the second anticipated the 1976 American Bicentennial. Each represented a time of historical awareness, however nostalgic, naïve or commercial, that led to renewed public enthusiasm for all things American. Our urban edifices are often built on a foundation of public optimism, as well as a concomitant trust in the plans of design professionals. In the case of Copley Square, that trust was rewarded with the creative works of three American architects of international stature and their three major landmark American architectural works: Trinity Church by H.H. Richardson; the Boston Public Library by Charles Follen McKim; and Hancock Tower by I.M. Pei, as well as by other talented architects and designers over time.

Richardson, McKim and Pei are among the most talented architects ever to design America. All were Americans with deep roots and personal experience in the international architectural advances of their day, of the Classical past and in important urban design developments throughout western history. The styles these major American architects have given us are so varied, moving in time from the monumental stone mass and weight of Trinity Church to the lightness and reflectivity of the glass of the Hancock Tower, that only through an understanding of the history and theory of architecture—of stylistic innovation over a century—can we truly appreciate the positive and mutually enhancing qualities of these architects' creations.

Tracing Historical Precedent

One of the most important threads this book will trace is the concept of historical precedent, or models, of style in architecture. An enduring visual memory of the fine work of our predecessors is found in buildings in Boston, demonstrating our American architecture to be part of the great tradition of Classical and European architecture. In this book, the author will suggest models, both well known and previously overlooked, for our Boston buildings.

The architecture of Copley Square in Boston also gives concrete testimony to the idea of the continuity of thought, of philosophy, of art, of architecture over space and time. We know that McKim's American masterpiece, the Boston Public Library, could not exist in its artistic form if not for the Renaissance of Rome and Florence. Copley as a public square would not likely exist as conscious urban form if not for London's Bloomsbury squares; and surely Commonwealth Avenue would look far less impressive if not for its recall of Paris's boulevards. We understand that this historic and modern American city, then, speaks to its European precedents while simultaneously recalling our shared and varied American roots.

Introduction

Historical precedent enriches the design of Copley Square, as seen here in the interior of the Boston Public Library.

Saving Significant Places

We in Boston, and our visitors, enjoy a kind of living urban museum of eighteenth- and nineteenth-century America on Beacon Hill, in the Boston Common and about the Public Garden. The Back Bay and Copley Square were comparatively historical latecomers to this colonial city, conceived in the nineteenth century. As twenty-first-century Americans, we are fortunate that excellent examples of our built history, from the seventeenth to the twentieth centuries, remain intact and in use.

The shared cultural patrimony of many American cities, towns and countryside is both celebrated and protected. It is important that we always keep in mind, though, that a city is a living thing, a growing and changing place. Stagnation in the name of preservation—or, conversely, destruction in the name of progress—is no longer an acceptable mode of urban planning. Only through careful balance (and by specifically defined status under historical preservation) can historical places maintain both modern life and the accretion of centuries in one contemporary city.

Introduction

Within the short constructed memory of the United States, the unique city of Boston is among the oldest and richest in architectural history, though of course, it is still youthful by European standards. Cities at their finest create a thoughtful blend of contemporary urban life with significant structures and streets of the past. America's built works are preserved by the listings in the National Register of Historic Places. There are approximately 80,000 listed places in America. The more rare designation of National Historic Landmark—of which there are approximately 2,500 sites—is reserved for truly unique historical and architectural sites.[1] A National Historic Landmark is one of the "places that emphasize a common bond between all Americans."[2]

Among those rare National Historic Landmarks—emphasizing only 3 percent of the properties in the National Register in the United States—Boston's Copley Square holds three major landmarks: Trinity Church by H.H. Richardson, the Boston Public Library by McKim, Mead & White and Old South Church by Cummings & Sears. The significant architectural sites of Boston's Copley Square in the Back Bay include:

NATIONAL HISTORIC LANDMARKS OF COPLEY SQUARE
Trinity Church (National Historic Landmark designation, 1970)
The Boston Public Library (National Historic Landmark designation, 1986)
Old South Church (National Historic Landmark designation, 1970)

NATIONAL REGISTER OF HISTORIC PLACES
Selected buildings and districts of Boston
Including all of the above, plus
Back Bay Historic District
(Charles River to Arlington Street, Boylston and Newbury Streets, listed 1973)
Beacon Hill Historic District (listed 1966)

HISTORIC HOTELS OF AMERICA
Fairmont Copley Plaza Hotel (named 1989)

Suggestions to the Reader: Sight and Sites

This book presents a broad introduction to an American urban place with its varied buildings, and to the streams of history that made those buildings and their European precedents. By its nature, it is wide ranging, from Boston

Introduction

history, to European Beaux-Arts architecture, to international urban design, to contemporary American architecture and urban design, all as illustrated by Copley Square.

There are individual studies available on particular buildings to be found, but rarely has Copley Square been studied as a complete and visually integrated site, an ensemble of buildings and landscape.

In a visual arts book such as this, this writer suggests that the reader always look to the illustrations first. This is your entrée into any visual arts book or any city—via sight and site. Next, feel free to skip about the text, as you would move about sectors of a city. Select the sections of an urban place, or your place in this book, that seem likely to be the most enlightening to you.

To weave together the chapters of a book, just as a city is woven of many threads, is the intention of this study. Thus, just as you would select a neighborhood to explore first in any new city, you may likewise select the topics in this book of most interest and perhaps even find areas of study new to you. For example:

If you are interested in historical Boston buildings and figures or historic preservation, the introduction and chapters 1, 2, 3, 4 and 7 will be good choices.

If investigating specific European precedents for architecture is your aim, consider chapters 2, 5, 8 and 10 for the author's speculations.

If urban design history of American and international cities is your interest, chapters 5, 6, 8, 9 and 10 and the conclusion will have meaning.

If the visual form and meaning of architecture as an art is your preference, chapters 5, 6, 8, 9 and 10 and the conclusion will be your choice.

Or, if you care about Copley Square and want to understand it fully as a place, observe the illustrations and consider reading the entire book!

It has required critical and continuous action through history to make Boston, based on both local and foreign models, into *architecture as ensemble*—historical yet alive, both massive and lightweight, geometric and irregular, contrasting and complementary, European and American, both antique and modern, all coalescing into a visual masterpiece and a humane place. (One must also acknowledge that some serious missteps in design have been made along the way and, in time, corrected.)

We are fortunate that the builders of Copley Square have enriched this city with a creative integration of form imbued with meaning and architectural gravitas. We will discover that Boston's Copley Square—under its trees, within its incessant movement of underground trolleys, long-distance Amtrak trains, MBTA buses, cars and bicycles and

Introduction

pedestrians—achieves something very special in the urban environment. In Copley Square, we discover not only the visual pleasures of place and a century of European-influenced architecture in America but also that exciting yet controlled sense of peaceful sanctuary amid urban chaos that we continue to seek in our cities.

CHAPTER 1

AMERICA

From Swamp to City Square

THE RIVER BEFORE THE SQUARE

Would it surprise you to learn that Bostonians walk on water? Yes, Copley Square with its massive structures, streets and sidewalks, indeed this entire sector of the city known today as Back Bay Boston, was once an ancient landscape of water and hills—specifically, three hills and a tidal estuary. "To the west [of the earliest site of Boston]…were the great reaches of mudflats and salt marshes which were covered by the tides at high water, known as the Back Bay; and beyond this the Charles River flowed down… as it approached Boston Harbor."[3]

Until the vast new urban planning and construction of the nineteenth-century city, a ten- to twenty-foot deep tidal estuary flowed freely and rhythmically. The river that currently divides the city of Boston from the city of Cambridge, Massachusetts, the Charles River, was once a changing marsh. The brackish waters over the early city rose and fell with the sea tides, the Charles River estuary moving constantly as it flowed forward and back through the land, eventually moving via Boston Harbor into the Atlantic Ocean.

The major developable land of early Boston consisted of topography very different from that which you may visit today. The original town was built about the harbor, there was very little actual land, water was everywhere, the tidal estuary ebbed and flowed daily and three glacial hills overlooked this

Copley Square

The Massachusetts State House, architect Charles Bulfinch (1798). This edifice is sited atop the topography of early Boston's Beacon Hill.

landscape. The Back Bay, where Copley Square now stands, was not even an aspiration. As an important early port city with one of the best American navigational links to England and France, Boston was always eager to keep its growth within striking distance of Boston Harbor.

At the time of the Revolution, there was far less Boston than stands today. The city of that time had been compared to a human hand with fingers—in other words, an arm of land reaching into a harbor, with a circle "fist" of land in the center, connected to the outside land only by a thin strip of land and a few bridges. Early Boston housing was built on what were then called the "Trimountain's Summits,"[4] for the city was composed of three significant hills: Beacon Hill, which we visit today; Mount Vernon, still remembered by the street named after it; and Cotton Hill, now barely a memory. It is surprising, even to Bostonians, to hear that our revered Beacon Hill, today a lone high point of the city, was once but one of a trio. The other rounded hills, composed of gravel, an ancient glacial moraine, were laid low. These hills of Boston were ignominiously destroyed, carried away in carts and dumped for fill into the Back Bay. This was Boston's forgotten topography.

Urban land is always a very valuable commodity…so why not make some more? Though land in early America seemed endless, land on a navigable river to a deep harbor, a direct route from America to Europe, was always prized and rare. Real estate with harbor access, like the shipping and trade that followed, became big business in Boston in the colonial era. After most of the natural hills of Boston were sold profitably as gravel, disposed of into the marshes along the Charles River, this historical natural tidal estuary was gone, its tides controlled. New dry, buildable and saleable land emerged. Thus, many of the distinguishing geological characteristics of Boston's topography were destroyed, but in their place arose the distinctive man-made urban forms of Boston's Back Bay, eventually including Commonwealth Avenue and Copley Square.

Further attempts to extend the city beyond the high land of Beacon Hill in time created such distinctive spaces as the Public Garden. Wooden pilings were sunk into the gravel, with land and buildings built up above it. Not only were the flat green spaces of the Garden added but also the mass and weight of rows of Back Bay mansions and sandstone churches, from the Arlington Street Church to Copley Square's Trinity Church. Below the city of today are the remnants of Boston's forgotten topography. "Trinity Church's location in Back Bay was originally a tidal mud flat. Great engineering feats were necessary to build a heavy stone church on filled land: Trinity Church rests on…wooden piles, each one pounded through 30 feet of gravel fill, silt and clay."[5]

We may be shocked to learn that the forefathers we were taught to revere for their ethics were sometimes disappointingly self-interested in their behavior toward their natural environment, viewing it as an exploitable commodity. As it has been described for us in Boston history, "Many were the laments over the action of the town…permitting it to be destroyed, and for many years thereafter the town fathers of that day were execrated as unpatriotic, materialistic vandals."[6]

The question arises: why would Bostonians engage in these complex feats of eighteenth- and nineteenth-century engineering? Why not just confine the city's future development to the extensive open land outside the city, to the west or north or south, on preexisting solid ground? The answer is found in the concept of connectivity to the deep water of the Atlantic Ocean. The connectivity to ships and port was crucial to colonial merchants. The connectivity of those ships to the globe was paramount. European trade thus drove the city to construct itself as close as possible to its route to the wider world, and that connection is via Boston Harbor.

Here is where America and Europe exchanged trade goods—and traded some good ideas.

Boston had become a significant commercial American port linking European with American mercantile interests in the eighteenth century. By the nineteenth century, the city was determined to evolve further as an aesthetically and intellectually impressive American city, in the style of those European places to which it had long been linked by its harbor. Boston's development has thus for centuries been an expression and a reflection of the currents of urban design and architectural style it has imported from Europe to America.

Building Early Boston

Long before "Copley" was even a place name, American artist John Singleton Copley (1738–1815) and American architect Charles Bulfinch (1763–1844) built the early city of Boston as we know it today. Copley and Bulfinch each held lands in Boston. On Beacon Hill, for example, there were "three houses which had belonged to John Singleton Copley, the painter, and in one of which he lived until his departure for England just prior to the Revolution."[7]

These early Bostonians, by profession artist and architect, also engaged in urban land development speculatively. Their artistic careers seemed to parallel their real estate interests: Copley, a portrait artist, favored individual residential houses; Bulfinch, an architect, developed multifamily attached brick row housing. Eventually, Copley sold his land to the Beacon Hill Proprietors, who developed his pasture as row housing; he would come to regret this deal. One of the least-known, and no longer extant, projects of early Boston was Bulfinch's Tontine Crescent development. The designs of these colonial row houses were strongly referential to the long, connected terraces and squares of row houses still found in London today.

Some early descendants of Patriots, including formerly patriotic families whose names are still remembered, were so eager to exploit the developable land opportunities around early Boston that, having cut down two hills equal to Beacon Hill, they built vigorously and extensively. Upon this newly created land was constructed, primarily for financial gain, the very Colonial architecture that we today consider "antique"

History through Architecture

The Royal Academy in London, where Copley studied history painting. The artist left America for England.

Boston, the Boston that we physically preserve in pristine condition—and in memory sacrosanct. In the words of one historical preservationist, "As we admire the red brick houses around Beacon Hill today, it is well to remember that to Bulfinch and…his contemporaries, these same houses connoted horrid crowding upon sites that had once been shaded by great trees where birds had sung, and made fragrant by the perfume of roses and honeysuckle."[8]

As was the privilege of their colonial wealth and education, both Copley and Bulfinch were extremely fortunate to be able to sail from Boston Harbor to European ports for purely personal enrichment, a rare experience for an American of their time. Through these early aficionados of European art and architecture, Boston acquired a taste for the sophisticated architecture and urban design of classical civilization, as well as of eighteenth-century London.

Copley in the Colony

John Singleton Copley, the Boston artist for whom Copley Square is named, had long painted in America. He was to become one of the first Americans to seek a serious cultural connection with Europe in the visual arts, traveling back and forth from Boston to London. While the Patriots he painted in America sought to throw off British rule, Copley was seeking the acceptance of the Royal Academy in Britain.

Thus, Copley Square, rather quizzically, takes its name not from a famous American Patriot but from a rare American who emigrated not from Europe to America but actually from Boston back to England. Perhaps this was due to that infamous tea that the Patriots (some of whose portraits he had likely painted) threw over the side of the ship in Boston Harbor; the Boston Tea Party was known to be connected to Copley's wife's family import business. Watching one's own valued trade goods going overboard may not have portended the best future for the Copley family in the colonies.

"Copley attempted to remain neutral during the prewar period, even though his father-in-law was the principal agent for the East India Company, owner of the ship from which the tea was dumped during the Boston Tea Party. With war imminent, Copley decided to leave for further study abroad. He had often expressed his desire to go—both to learn from and to test himself against European artists.…He sailed on June 10, 1774, never to return. His departure symbolized the end of the colonial era in American art."[9]

Beyond the ominous message in the tea leaves, there was an artistic reason for Copley to depart Boston as well. Copley understood that he was an isolated colonial American painter, yet one with aspirations to be accepted by European artistic circles, particularly by the British artists of the time. He thus submitted a sample of his work to the Royal Academy of Art in London for comment by Sir Joshua Reynolds. Copley sent his favorite painting, the heartfelt *Boy with a Squirrel*, now in the Boston Museum of Fine Arts, to London, to the Royal Academy. The academy's critical comments were essentially that though Copley's work displayed natural talent—with a colonial lack of sophistication perhaps implied—he would need to become more worldly in his style.

Copley needed, in his mind, the approval and critique of Sir Joshua Reynolds, respected portrait painter and head of the Royal Academy, to legitimize his outsider American work. Thus, he took the words of his chosen mentor perhaps too deeply to heart. Many art historians have felt that Copley lost the freshness of his colonial native inborn talent through the strictures he self-imposed after his European visit to the Royal Academy. A great interpreter of American Patriots, including Paul Revere and John Adams, Copley himself was always ambivalent about his American commitments.

Copley in the Academy

A step upward in the arts, for Copley at least, required study in England to reach his artistic potential internationally. Art at this time was highly structured and class-oriented. The artistic hierarchy of the Royal Academy valued artworks by importance of subject matter, in the following order, from very valuable to less so: works of mythological and religious figures; history painting of important scenes and battles; portraits of important persons; landscapes; genre painting of everyday persons and scenes. Copley could thus understand that his actually very insightful portraits of Americans might not be considered sufficiently sophisticated beyond the colonies.

Perhaps still harboring that sinking feeling from the Tea Party affair, plus his now believing the critique of the Royal Academy, on one hand, versus his thriving colonial portrait business, plus his real estate holdings on Beacon Hill, on the other, Copley vacillated back and forth between America and England for years. Ultimately, even after great success in Boston, he chose to emigrate and to resettle with his family in London permanently. Socially, this may have been a good decision for Copley, as now he could paint not just simple colonials and American Patriots but also British aristocrats and even perhaps members of the Royal Family. But artistically, it is generally agreed that this was a sad loss of his fresh American talent. Gone was the simplicity and innocence of the *Boy with a Squirrel*, replaced with the drapery and increasing artistic pretenses of his later British portraits.

Regrettably, Copley sacrificed something very original and very American in himself and his work to ingratiate himself into higher European social circles artistically. It is suggested that visitors to Copley Square may also wish to visit the Boston Museum of Fine Arts in the Fenway sector of the city to make the comparison of American Copley and European-influenced Copley for themselves. It is also notable to recall that Copley Square was at first the site of the Museum of Fine Arts, home of a major collection of Copley's work. A number of Copley's portraits are exhibited there, as well as in Burlington House, London, home of the Royal Academy, the place to which Copley so aspired.[10]

Ultimately, as the Revolutionary War approached, Copley, painter of American Patriots, chose to leave his Beacon Hill home and extensive properties to live with his family full time in London, never to return to America. It is certainly a strangeness of Boston history that we have named one of our nationally known urban centers after one of the few Americans who actually left America permanently and emigrated backward—from America to England. There could be found an implied cultural rejection of Boston, even of America, here, if we chose to discover it rather than to celebrate it. We, however, remember John Singleton Copley with colonial nostalgia as a figure whose name is forever honored in a place that did not exist in his lifetime. We choose in Copley to celebrate a Bostonian who did not think Boston was quite sophisticated enough for his art. In spite of his personal ambivalence, we celebrate Copley, in his own Copley Square, today in America.

Art Square to Copley Square

We Americans still have Copley's freshest and finest paintings in our collections, including the moving portraits he painted of our greatest Patriots, John Hancock and Paul Revere, at the Boston Museum of Fine Arts. And of course, his latter-day namesake, Copley Square, is ours to enjoy every day. It is an irony of American history that the land under the square now named after Copley was not even there, except as a swamp, in his lifetime. A statue of Copley[11] stands there today, paint brush in hand, overlooking, perhaps in amazement, the square where he never stood—because it did not exist in his lifetime. John Singleton Copley, in spite of his own lifelong ambivalence toward America, was certainly the greatest of the American colonial painters, and thus it seems fitting that a major historical crossroads of Boston should recall—and cause us as spectators to recall—his American artistic vision.

Art, architecture and history have all been of note in Boston's Copley Square. This place of famed architecture had been associated with art from its building. Originally called "Art Square," as the early location of the Boston Museum of Fine Arts, "Copley Square" was the amended name that was given to this place and remains today, after the museum moved from this

The gates of the Public Garden, Back Bay, Boston, a short walk from Copley Square.

square to the then newly developing sector of Boston known as the Fenway, where it is located today.

Copley Square, or Art Square, has not always behaved at all pristinely in its approach to preservation—and for that we might sometimes be grateful. What were lost were fairly commonplace Victorian buildings. For example, at the turn of the century, the Museum of Fine Arts occupied the site of the current Copley Plaza Hotel. Near it was a Victorian building for the food importer S.S. Pierce. The museum building of the time by Sturgis and Brigham (1876–1911) was Victorian Gothic, with pointed arches above a heavy brick polychrome mass. This early building was razed in 1911, as the museum moved from Copley Square to its more mature Beaux-Arts Classical Revival home in Fenway.

Other changes to historical buildings have occurred over time in Copley Square. Old South Church, for example, appears to have had changes of mind over time about the interiors of their own Venetian Gothic décor.[12] This church, however, like the art museum, persisted in its search for excellence in design, and what we find today is the outcome of reconsidered and renewed understanding of ecclesiastical design.

Copley Square, the place, has achieved what Copley, the man, could not—an authentic American experience on American soil, yet strongly influenced by European style. Within this special place, Copley Square, today we find an impressive and nationally celebrated collection of historical and contemporary American architecture. "History is not static....Cities have an evolving history representing many time periods."[13] Copley Square and its Boston environs continue to engage in this past-present dynamic. The London-like squares of eighteenth-century Beacon Hill and the nineteenth-century Parisian-influenced Back Bay boulevards around Copley Square together reflect the past-to-present continuum of this place.

CHAPTER 2

AMERICA TO EUROPE

Americans Discover Antiquity

THE GRAND TOUR: BOSTON TO LONDON TO PARIS TO ROME TO BOSTON

Early Bostonians were only one or two generations removed from Europe, its culture and its cities, and thus, Bostonians of influence heard of the wider world and were strongly motivated to re-create their own sophisticated European-influenced city right here in the American colony of Boston. There were virtually no professional architects found in America. Eighteenth-century illustrated books on antiquities were published but rare. Georgian and Federal designs were based on pattern books from which carpenters and builders learned.

The Grand Tour of the eighteenth and nineteenth centuries was a privilege of the upper class and the educated—the wealthy (male) intelligentsia of the era. Boston was home to many of the American intelligentsia, educated, erudite and necessarily wealthy, of their day. President Thomas Jefferson had traveled from London to Paris, even as far as Nimes in the South of France, to view the Classical Roman architecture of the Maison Carrée, an ancient temple in the French city. Some travelers ventured even farther into Italy and Greece for the inspiration of the ancient Roman and Greek civilizations. Boston portrait artist John Singleton Copley studied in London; Thomas Jefferson had lived in Paris. Boston architect Charles Bulfinch wrote to Thomas Jefferson for itinerary suggestions and followed Jefferson's lead on his own Grand Tour of Europe.

Copley Square

An etching, an example of an Italian *veduta*, or travel illustration, collected by Americans on the Grand Tour during the eighteenth and nineteenth centuries, unsigned. *Collection of the author.*

There were even early "postcards" to be collected on the Grand Tour. Known as the *vedute* or "views," these prints were small scenic etchings on paper, generally of the architectural sites and ruins of Italy or the South of France, to collect to take home to show your friends and family left behind in the colonies. These simple prints were to become inspirations to American architecture, introducing Classical and Renaissance forms into the American visual vocabulary. Examples of these simple illustrated works, showing the Italian cities of Siena and Florence, are included in this book.

The major artist and architect of the colonial American period, John Singleton Copley and Charles Bulfinch, were among the fortunate few to make the Grand Tour. Architecture was a profession of a gentleman, and by that was meant mannered, though not necessarily gentle or even well mannered. It implied class rather than behavior. It appears, however, that both Copley and Bulfinch were "gentlemen" in every sense of the word. It also helped one's architectural ambitions in the eighteenth and nineteenth centuries to be born into a prominent Boston landholding family with a significant name, to marry well and to have influential friends.

These artistic gentlemen were well educated in America, but as colonials, they lacked the credentials of first-person European site exploration. Thus, via different paths, each set about creating the cachet of true European artistic "class." One of the rare marks of the educated gentleman, the patina that separated an American native from a man of the world, was first-person European travel to authentic architectural sites of the ancient world.

The Grand Tour meant sailing from America—in their cases from Boston—for six months to a year of traveling about Europe, from London or Paris, to the South of France, to Rome, about Italy and even, rarely, to

History through Architecture

Greece. It was a difficult horse and carriage journey, fraught with danger, excitement and even highwaymen, with few developed roads, prohibitively expensive for most. Historic places that we today might not expect to be so difficult to visit, such as the Forum Romanum, were nearly forgotten and very isolated then, even overgrown with vines, as seen in Piranesi prints of the day.

Only through this pilgrimage, and its ensuing insight into significant cultural sites, though, could an American-born artist or architect truly be expected to comprehend the forms and meaning of antiquity and of eighteenth-century Europe. John Singleton Copley, in particular, traveled extensively throughout Europe and spent a great deal of time living in London. Bulfinch sought out Jefferson, American architect and intellectual as his architectural mentor, and with a letter of introduction from Jefferson, who had been American ambassador to France, began his own Grand Tour. Thus, Boston architect Bulfinch followed, quite literally, in the footsteps of Thomas Jefferson, third president of the United States of America.

As Copley had spent the Revolution in England, decades later, during the American Civil War, it would be another artist of Copley Square, architect H.H. Richardson, who would leave America for Europe for the duration. It appears, as is often the case in history, that privilege, politics, money and social connections were protective in some very difficult times. These benefits of class have often played a role in the lives of Americans who have been able to travel and, thus, to escape conflict at home for cultural enlightenment and safety from turbulence.

American architects of the nineteenth century considered their work to be an aesthetic continuity with the greatest works of the past, particularly of the Classical and European past. The importation of European style to an earlier Boston defined the city for decades. In the great tradition of eighteenth-century American artists and thinkers seeking European precedents, from Jefferson to Bulfinch to Copley, nineteenth-century architects Richardson and McKim, too, brought to their American works the knowledge of the significant buildings of Europe. These influences came to America via the Grand Tour and *vedute*, travel sketches of important sites, the postcards of the era, as well as in the more sophisticated illustrated architectural books of engravings that were then being published.

Antiquity, Architectural Precedent and the Appropriateness of Form

The use of architectural precedent in the eighteenth, nineteenth and early twentieth centuries was based on the proper, or "appropriate," choice of forms from the historical past to express the symbolic meaning of the architecture of the present. Certainly, many complex and contradictory aesthetic questions of style and of the "appropriateness of form" would have been debated in Boston during the construction of Copley Square. The rounded arch, for example, with its complex history, was dispersed as structure and decorative form from Rome throughout Europe and eventually to America. However, was it "appropriate" to use a Roman or pre-Christian "pagan" structure for a church? This was the kind of question architecture once debated.

The pagan forms of Rome, with stone arches and arcades, might be thought of as one very early, though contradictory, precedent for the decorative arches we find today in many Christian churches, including Boston's Trinity Church. The structural and decorative form of the arch had persisted from Roman antiquity into early Christian Romanesque churches, especially in France. Thus, a previously "pagan" form had already been accepted by the Church long before it moved to Copley Square. Antiquity became "appropriate" for modern American architecture as forms and meanings were transferred and transformed.

Two landmarks of Copley Square, Trinity Church and the Boston Public Library, creatively express the historical continuity of the arch of Classical antiquity, from the Roman Colosseum, to French Romanesque churches, to Italian Renaissance palaces, to nineteenth-century Boston buildings, on their façades facing Copley Square. Artistic use of motifs of architecture of the past by the Beaux-Arts was discussed by art historian Arthur Drexler: "Some… problems, among them the question of how to use the past, may perhaps be seen now as possibilities that are liberating rather than constraining."[14]

The close observer will note when walking about this urban square in Boston that the rounded arch, both as structure and as decoration, has become in Copley Square an often-echoed form. First seen here in Richardson's Trinity Church, soon also to be found on the façade of McKim's Boston Public Library and, even a century later, in the structure of Boston's contemporary Back Bay Station, the architecture of Copley Square pays homage to the rounded arch and, via the repetition of this motif, to the architecture of antiquity.

L'École des Beaux-Arts in Paris

A few fortunate Americans learned the European architectural antecedents for their own work both informally, via personal European travel, and formally, via a European architectural education. H.H. Richardson was among the first Americans to attend the prestigious Parisian architectural institution L'École des Beaux-Arts— literally, the School of Fine (or Beautiful) Arts. Following Richardson's example, generations of American architectural students, impressed with his French education, enrolled in this internationally premier architectural academy on the Left Bank of Paris. Forever after, an architect would be known as being "École" educated. This rigorous training in the history of the arts, in architectural precedent, in the building plan as a sequence of spaces and in architecture as the continuity of the highest expression of the Classical traditions of Greece and Rome, would distinguish many of the greatest architects of the late nineteenth and early twentieth centuries in Europe and America.

Beaux-Arts architecture in France, with Corinthian columns derived from Classical architecture.

Many important architectural firms in America were derived from these École associations. The premier American Beaux-Arts architectural firm was McKim, Mead & White, New York partners who would become the architects of the Boston Public Library, the Rhode Island State Capitol and the Morgan Library in New York. Other well-known École-trained architects included the New York firm of Carrere & Hastings, designers of the New York Public Library; and the Boston firm of Cummings and Sears, designers of Old South Church in Copley Square. The European-influenced design of L'École des Beaux-Arts in the nineteenth century became the style setter for major public institutions such as libraries, museums and city halls in major American cities, as we will see in Boston, as well as in New York City, Washington, D.C., San Francisco, Chicago and many other significant American cities.

An American Critique of the Beaux-Arts Style

None of the historic American spaces of Copley Square have stagnated into faux urban antiques. They continue to support modern life within our historical environment, historical landmarks with insightful modern design as well as landscape, integrated to create this dynamic contemporary city. The physical character of Copley Square has seen iterations of landscape architecture design and redesign for the plantings and hardscape. Fortunately, today, we have grass and trees rather than the asphalt and concrete too often found in urban open spaces. Even a tall building, a glass skyscraper, has been integrated into this historical context.

This square has evolved over time toward improvement. It must be noted, however, that there was at least one critical voice speaking against the coming of European style to America, who advocated early for a true American style not based in ancient or European precedent. That voice belonged to one of the most important Early Modern architects in America: Chicago architect Louis Sullivan (born 1856 in Boston, died 1924 in Chicago), author of the groundbreaking essay "The Tall Building Artistically Considered."

In the often-quoted essay in which Sullivan gave us the fundamental insight into design "Form ever follows function," he likewise, though less famously, commented, "When our architects shall cease strutting…vainglorious in the asylum of a foreign school…and strangling bonds of the schools cannot stifle…us…when it becomes evident that we are merely speaking a foreign language with a noticeable American accent…then it may be proclaimed that…architecture…will soon become a fine art in the true…sense of the word." Louis Sullivan published his very insightful, critical and emotional essay in 1896—within a year of the opening of McKim, Mead & White's very French-influenced work in Copley Square, the Boston Public Library, a building that certainly could be said to be "speaking a foreign language."[15]

International Ideals in Stone and Glass

Trinity Church, the Boston Public Library and the glass skyscraper known as the Hancock Tower; these three significant buildings bear the visual weight and meaning of Copley Square. In the view of this author, they stand for long traditions of European and American experience: Church, State and

History through Architecture

Back Bay of Boston, Commonwealth Avenue. *Tichnor Brothers Post Card Collection, Boston Public Library, Massachusetts Collections Online, Digital Commonwealth.*

Commerce; or perhaps: Faith, Reason and Necessity. They speak to the historical forms of Antiquity in counterpoint to the contemporary. They stand like ancient stone centurions over the open space of Copley Square.

We will examine the components of this place through its historic landmarks and listed buildings, considering them as an ensemble or complementary artistic grouping: Trinity Church and the Boston Public Library, as well as Old South Church and the Copley Plaza Hotel, moving into selected antiques of tomorrow. To understand the living architectural complements of Copley Square, we will look to the buildings that complete the urban ensemble of Boston's Copley Square and then on to its famed Modern design in glass, the Hancock Tower.

These buildings of Copley Square represent architecture in its historical and modern aesthetic creativity: mass, weight, light, complexity, structure, ornament, simplicity of form, stone and glass and steel. They together represent unmoving constructions amid incessant movement of transit and pedestrians. They are modern symbols of the ancient philosophies of the active and the contemplative life, and of the legacy of the Arts and Sciences.

The panoply of their styles together represents all the prevailing emotions of the eras of their designs: cool Classical architecture versus emotive picturesque edifices. We will explore the historical architectural ideas and antique precedents, as well as the urban realities of our modern city, and how all these themes not only coexist but actually enliven one another. We will watch as this place evolves in style and meaning over a century. We will take our own Grand Tour of the active urban space and enduring international architecture of Copley Square.

CHAPTER 3

AMERICA

An Evolving Environment

THE CHANGING CONFIGURATIONS OF COPLEY SQUARE

The heritage of Boston's Copley Square has been preserved as a public legacy within its historical architectural forms. To appreciate this place as it stands today, it is important to trace the physical concept of the urban configuration that defines Copley Square. The shape of Copley Square was not always square or even rectangular; to the contrary, it was previously a kind of triangle, a crossing point for pedestrians amid bus and trolley traffic. That triangle, known as a square, was not yet called "Copley" Square, as we know it today, after the colonial artist. This place was at first more generically known as "Art" Square.

Four streets currently form the square, actually more of a rectangle: the primary commercial avenue, running east–west, named Boylston Street; its smaller parallel street, St. James Avenue; and, at right angles to Boylston Street, the cross streets, Clarendon Street and Dartmouth Street, the first near Trinity Church and the other fronting the Boston Public Library. These four streets set Copley Square at the southern edge, but still within the grid, of Boston's historic Back Bay. To understand the place called "Copley" as a "Square," we will explore how it moved from one geometric shape to another.

At one time, a major cross-town street, Huntington Avenue, cut across these streets diagonally, so traffic ran quickly through the pedestrian

Copley Square with Trinity Church. *Tichnor Brothers Post Card Collection, Trinity Church, Massachusetts Collections Online, Digital Commonwealth.*

square. Complicating the configuration of this place was the meeting of two unmatched street grids, that of the Back Bay of Boston meeting the grid of the South End of Boston. It was not until the 1960s that the organization of the rectangular configuration was complete. This was a complex process of urban evolution, diverting traffic for the benefit of pedestrians and moving the city toward respect for public pedestrian open space.

Perhaps the lesson learned is that our cities are not, and never have been, historical museums; nor should they be simply two-dimensional graph paper plans for mercenary economic development. We must, therefore, make every effort to judge the physical planning of the city with educated intuition for the present as well as for the future. We should think of the design of the city as a tapestry, considering the long-term value and meaning of the place and its component architectural parts, or threads.

If we think of a city as composed of an "urban fabric" of interwoven textural threads, we may realize that a thoughtless tear in one place affects the entity. Boston and all American cities must remain living exponents of human interaction, endeavor and human hopes. The physical structure that creates the warp and weft of its urban fabric is the interweaving of

History through Architecture

the street patterns. In Boston's planned Back Bay, the gridded pattern of this "fabric" is easily identifiable because it represents logical space within a less rational city.

When Copley Square was created in the mid-nineteenth century, the older grid of the South End sector of the city converged with the new grid of the Back Bay here, at an angle. Therefore, the area was a transitional space from one existing Boston neighborhood to a new neighborhood, always a crossroads. It was both an interruption of the street patterns and a meeting place, both a break in the city and, conversely, a connection. This oppositional meaning gives dynamism to places that break the street patterns—if, and only if, they are well handled by planners and architects.

Copley Square began to come together as a defined public place in the late nineteenth century, with the renaming of the cross roads as we now know it as "Copley Square" in 1895.[16] Simultaneous with the name change were the architectural changes to the place. In essence, Copley Square in the last decades of the nineteenth century was becoming a defined and memorable American place—with a European flavor. Though many major physical transformations have been made over a century, the basic intent and architectural landmarks—the churches and the library—of this place endure.

There have been conscious efforts, by the City of Boston and by volunteer organizations, to make this place an active pedestrian space. Boylston Street maintains a good mix of commercial storefronts that keep the city lively, and these commercial buildings are basically well proportioned for the street life and look. A competition to design the public space of the square was won in 1965 by Sasaki Dawson DeMay Associates; the current green configuration is the result of a 1983 competition-winning work of Dean Abbot of Clarke & Rapuano, Inc. The contemporary design is respectful of the landmarks and landscape, functional physically for pedestrians and inviting to the public.[17]

We will follow the historical development of the international shape of the urban pedestrian square, from Rome and Paris and London eventually here to Boston and to other American cities' designs. This is the urban history that landmarks and our streets and squares tell. But first, some Boston observations to notice as you walk in this city.

Copley Square

Some "Common" Boston Place Names

"Copley Square" is correctly spelled and pronounced with a short "o." Though there were rare colonial misspellings of this name, as a place, today Copley always sounds like a "copse" of trees or like "copper." Certain city places are always—in historical Bostonian or current Boston-speak—defined as singular, in every sense of the word: "the Public Garden" or "the Boston Common." Note that here in Boston, there is never an "s" on either "Garden" or "Common," and "the" is all one needs to define one's location. However, for some reason long forgotten, Bostonians say simply "Symphony" but never "the Symphony." People here do not take "the subway"; they take the "T" (one assumes this refers to "trolley" or public "transit," but that is never really explained to visitors). So it might be said, "I will take the T from the Common to Symphony."

Also of note, especially when walking as a pedestrian around Boston, is the fact that the north–south streets of Back Bay, from the Public Garden to Massachusetts Avenue, in an unexpected bit of Boston-applied logic, are arranged alphabetically: Arlington Street, Berkeley Street, Clarendon Street, Dartmouth Street, Exeter Street, Fairfield Street, Gloucester Street, Hereford Street. Copley Square is found between Clarendon and Dartmouth Streets. To the north, Copley Square is bordered by the major commercial street of the Back Bay, Boylston Street, and on the south by the quieter St. James Avenue.

Via the active public transit hub of Copley Square, you can catch the T to the Boston Common or connect to Harvard Yard in Cambridge. You can even take the Amtrak train from Copley Square direct to the modern skyscrapers of New York City or to the Neo-Classical monuments of Washington, D.C.

Copley is active all day, all seasons. Ice art is sculpted here on New Year's Eve; fresh vegetables are sold at an outdoor market. The hotels are alive, the shops and restaurants are open day to night. Pedestrians walk from one city place to another, living a car-free urban life here, with good connections to many American sites at their doors.

Boston Celebrates Itself—Often

Many celebrations can be found amid confetti falling in Copley Square. Bostonians have traditionally celebrated and proudly shared their contributions to American history, as well as their own very Boston-ness via their quirky holidays. Americans know well the traditional televised Boston Fourth of July fireworks celebrations, but there are others. The fall brings Columbus Day weekend for autumn colors of trees and college crew team colors rowing on the river. The Head of the Charles Regatta displays scores of sleek vessels, sculls and crew shells, adding color and movement to the Charles River landscape later in the fall for an international rowing competition.

The most famous specifically Bostonian holiday is Patriots' Day, a Monday in April, a celebration of the American Revolution. It has become synonymous with the running of the Boston Marathon, now informally called Marathon Monday.[18] This contemporary race actually represents an ancient Greek tradition and thus is very much in keeping with the historical and architectural Classical meaning of Copley Square. The finish line is painted in front of the Johnson Building of the Boston Public Library. The Boston Marathon completes its twenty-six-mile run here.

The Boston Marathon is a joyous ancient tradition in Boston, still celebrated after one hundred years. It began also as a "transfer" from Europe, not as built form but as transfer of tradition: the word "Marathon" refers to a city in ancient Greece. Marathon had its roots in Greek antiquity as a much-respected intellectual and artistic, as well as athletic, civilization and a model for the late nineteenth-century Beaux-Arts artists, architects, designers and intellectuals who created Copley Square. Always historically appropriate, Boston has named even its favorite public sporting event after an ancient Classical civilization.

Today, the Marathon finish line is painted on the pavement just west of Copley Square proper, so yes, that is the Johnson Building of the Boston Public Library that you see in the background of pictures of exhausted runners crossing the line. This is a fitting visual association of a winning event with a successfully designed site: the Boston Marathon, first raced in 1897, began in Boston close in time to the opening of the Boston Public Library.

Bostonians still compliment themselves on their city's sending the British on the run out of their Massachusetts Bay Colony with their own special holiday, observed only in the Commonwealth, called Evacuation Day, an admittedly odd name for a holiday. Boston does not only celebrate its British-aimed holidays of Patriots' Day, Evacuation Day and the Fourth of July, however; it even has had its own French-themed holiday. Lafayette Day in May was intended to celebrate the Revolutionary assistance of the

Marquis. Bostonians particularly enjoy dancing in the streets on their own very French Back Bay Bastille Day.

There are also serious commemorative days specific in the city's history. On Crispus Attucks Day, "community leaders" of Boston "publicly celebrate the important contributions of black citizens throughout American history…and organized Boston's first Crispus Attucks Day in March 1858 to commemorate the black man who was among the five slain by the British during the Boston Massacre."[19]

THE CONSTITUTION AND SOCIAL CAUSES CONSIDERED

Here across a wide green lawn, Church faces State, in the forms of Trinity Church and the Boston Public Library. No better American symbolic architectural statement of the First Amendment can be found than this private church facing this public library; no better example than this one in Boston can be built of the historical concepts of faith versus reason. This square, embodied by Trinity Church and the Boston Public Library, speaks forever of the foundational American concept of the separation of church and state. Massachusetts, once the home of Pilgrims, here brought to life the modern Jeffersonian principles that inform our everyday American life. Copley Square thus remains a physical manifestation of the United States Constitution, the ideals conceived and codified for the creation of our country.

Though specifically fulfilling a major commission for the Episcopal Church, Trinity Church is also an important Boston building in a very public place. Though particularly remembered for this commission, "Richardson was not by choice a church builder."[20] With this landmark Boston church, however, Richardson here made a universal and lasting statement on the concept of religion and social justice in America. As the church faces the public square, it both embraces and distinguishes itself from the public space of the city, recognizing the place of religion in America.

Plans were drawn for the private, religious home of Trinity Church to face a newly commissioned major public, secular edifice, the Boston Public Library, across Copley Square. Major American democratic values would hereafter be symbolized in the stones of this square. Reading and education would be equated with American freedom. The architecture and design of

Copley Square with the Boston Public Library. *Tichnor Brothers Post Card Collection, Boston Public Library, Massachusetts Collections Online, Digital Commonwealth.*

the Boston Public Library "bear witness to the dedication and trust of a citizenry who believed in the raison d'etre of the public library, that it was 'built by the people and dedicated to the advancement of learning.'"[21]

Here, too, abolitionist history took form in Richardson's church and McKim's library. In the eighteenth century, Boston had fought valiantly for freedom for the colonies—freedom from oppression, from unrepresentative government, from royalty, from European domination. In the nineteenth century, Boston fought for the promise of freedom for all, through the fight for the most significant freedom: the freedom from slavery.

Freedom and justice have always been motivating themes of Boston, as the city became one of the leading sites in the nation, first in revolution and then in abolition, as historian Berensen makes clear: "Massachusetts was the first state to abolish slavery."[22] The architect of Trinity Church, Louisiana-born H.H. Richardson, came from a slaveholding family, but as an adult, he followed the abolitionist path. Richardson was in the circle of the pastor of Trinity Church, the Reverend Phillips Brooks, an active abolitionist orator of Trinity whose antislavery sermons were said to be passionate. Charles McKim, architect of the Boston Public Library, married into a Quaker abolitionist family, bringing social conscience, as well as insightful design for public access to ideas through library books, into Copley Square.

Copley Square has over time represented the most significant progressive causes and events of Boston history—eighteenth- and nineteenth-century ideas on religion, state, abolitionism, public education through books, as well as twentieth-century antiwar rallies and environmental movements. Further, the youth volunteers of AmeriCorps City Year have met here for morning reveille before going off to work long days to improve inner-city classrooms and public urban sites. Massachusetts Senator Ted Kennedy spoke inspiringly to hundreds of youthful AmeriCorps City Year Corps members here in Copley Square. As it has been for those idealistic young City Year volunteers, Copley Square continues its role as an open-air rallying place for social meaning and change in modern Boston, both past and present. It is still a place to be, a destination for real urban activities. The library is both welcoming and functional. The churches are socially participatory. Copley Square is a shared public forum.

Copley Square is an aesthetic embodiment, not only of architectural styles but also of nineteenth- and twentieth-century moral and intellectual American ideas and ideals. Constitutional principles of Jeffersonian democracy are illustrated here in built urban form. This place is a physical expression of America and a place where the public has gathered for decades to examine and to demand the ideas of a more just, peaceful and equal America. Though this physical environment has evolved over time, the American ideals represented in Copley Square remain.

CHAPTER 4

AMERICA

The Societal Significance of Trinity Church

Do but build large enough, and carve boldly enough, and all the world will hear you; they cannot choose but to look.[23]

Trinity Church, for Boston, is a symbol not only of the Anglican religion but also of Boston within American history, of bravery shown for ethical causes, of famous oration, particularly concerning the abolition of slavery, "service to the community" and "pastoral care."[24] This building symbolically speaks to the stances on social justice that institutions have traditionally taken in Boston.

Trinity Church was the first great institution to locate within the new Copley Square. Here in Copley Square, the new Trinity Church became a physical symbol of its ecclesiastical and societal meaning and, in the process, set a new American style for public buildings. Key figures were Reverend Phillips Brooks, architect H.H. Richardson and British art theorist John Ruskin, whose words above echo today in Copley Square.

In the words of architectural historian Keith N. Morgan, "The young Phillips Brooks was called to the local pulpit in 1869. He quickly set in motion a series of initiatives that made Trinity Church the most dynamic religious institution in the city.…The most tangible of Brooks's visions was to move the church from its early nineteenth-century quarters…to a larger and more visible site in the expanding Back Bay."[25] Reverend Brooks brought his college friend and colleague H.H. Richardson, an architect who reflected Ruskin's thoughts, into the Trinity design.

The towers, turrets and cross of Trinity Church.

How perfect a theoretical and artistic foundation is found for Brooks and Richardson's ecclesiastical vision in the lectures and writings of then contemporary British art scholar John Ruskin, whose association of art with morality was widely respected at the time of the inception of this church project. Acknowledged to be the most influential stylistically for Richardson were the Romanesque churches that he had visited and sketched in France. To this observer, however, the panoply of motifs that Richardson employed at Trinity appears to be more wide ranging than solely French Romanesque. Creative influences can also be observed ranging from Ruskinian English, to ancient Celtic, to Venetian, all visually expressed in America with a British "accent," or interpretation.

Any number of design motifs may have been recalled by a nineteenth-century architect. It is likely that Richardson was thinking of Venetian styles, with a contemporary British interpretation, when he designed his Trinity Church—and invented the new and original American architectural style we still call "Richardsonian Romanesque." Richardson "represented the spirit of the age, a spirit that wanted to present itself boldly to the world….Richardsonian Romanesque architecture became an almost universal prototype for public buildings and was often used for churches, libraries, train stations, and other large institutional structures."[26]

Following his European sojourns, Richardson's lifetime of American architectural commissions began with his winning the competition for Trinity Church in Copley Square. What we see today in Trinity is a summation of Richardson's European travel, his French École education, his study of British architectural theory and an introduction of his own personal and original direction for American architecture. For a major Christian church with a significant artistic program, within a primary American cultural city, with his religious colleague, Richardson honed thought into architectural form, as he created a landmark building in a major public square in America.

This is a meaningful edifice for America. It is a place for religious practice but also a place for pedestrians to rest in the city, to sit contemplatively on the sandstone front steps, under the stone arches, enjoying the slanting afternoon winter sun. As Ruskin wrote in his commentary on the arts, "lastly, and chiefly, you must love the creatures to whom you minister, your fellow men."[27]

Trinity Church was named a National Historic Landmark in 1971.

Selected Artists and Thinkers of Trinity Church

H.H. Richardson, Architect of the Richardsonian Romanesque Style

Henry Hobson Richardson (1838–1886) is known to us as a primary force in mid- to late nineteenth-century American architecture. He brought European historical architectural vision to his uniquely original American style. His European sojourn and studies became very influential in his American works in the Northeast, where he creatively melded these sources with his understanding of the natural materials of America. Richardson went on, after the Trinity Church commission, to become one of the most influential American architects of all time. His powerful style and sense of materials and form is without peer, displaying the eternal relationship of architecture to nature.

A transplant to the intellectual circles of Boston, a native of Louisiana, Richardson had spent the years of the American Civil War in France, studying at the École des Beaux-Arts in Paris. In Europe, he was moved artistically by the early Medieval and Romanesque basilicas he sketched in the provinces of France. Richardson additionally collected books of European architectural illustrations. American students of art and architecture continued the educational traditions begun by Richardson throughout the nineteenth and early twentieth centuries, via European travel and study and by collecting illustrated books. His firm employed both Charles Follen McKim and Stanford White as draftsmen early in their architectural careers, before they formed their own firm that was twenty years later to design the Boston Public Library, across Copley Square.

In addition to Trinity Church, readers may also wish to see selections of Richardson's architecture, or the Richardsonian style, at the following places in New England: Brattle Square Church, Commonwealth Avenue, Back Bay, Boston; Sever Hall, Harvard Yard, Harvard University, Cambridge, Massachusetts; Stoughton House, Brattle Street, Cambridge, Massachusetts; Stonehurst Estate, Waltham, Massachusetts, with landscape architect Frederick Law Olmsted; and train stations at Wellesley Hills and Wellesley Farms, Massachusetts.

Reverend Phillips Brooks, Rector

The selection of site and designer is fundamental to good architecture, and the Reverend Phillips Brooks (1835–1893) chose both the newly planned Copley Square as the site of his church and H.H. Richardson as the architect. Moving his old downtown church to the newly developed Copley Square was a prescient act of urban planning, and choosing Richardson as the architect was perhaps the most influential aesthetic decision ever to be made in Copley Square history. Thanks to Brooks, a very high standard for buildings was set. Brooks and Richardson, Harvard men, traveled together to England, France and Italy in the 1880s viewing early Christian churches and ancient architecture.

Education; a shared liberal viewpoint, including on abolition; and a lifelong mutual respect between rector and architect resulted in the powerful plans for a major American church project for Trinity Church. An important student nonprofit organization is now named after the Reverend Phillips Brooks. Many good works in his name are accomplished today by Phillips Brooks House of Harvard University. A statue of Phillips Brooks by sculptor Augustus Saint-Gaudens (1848–1907) stands outside Trinity Church.

Professor John Ruskin, Theorist of British (and Venetian) Influences

"All forms, and ornaments, and images, have a moral meaning as well as a natural one."[28] These words were written about St. Mark's, Venice, as a late coda to words that Oxford University's Slade Professor of Art John Ruskin (1819–1900) had been writing on the architecture of Venice since 1849. In his published treatises and lectures, including his landmark book *The Stones of Venice* (1851) and his book on his instructions for architects, *Seven Lamps of Architecture* (1849), Ruskin dictated that the aesthetics of architecture were to be integrated with a very strong moral code.

The architect, in Ruskin's world, was raised to the level of the moral thinker and expressive artist and even to a kind of benevolent paternalistic figure—almost a religious one. The architect followed "lamps," or lights of morality. The "Seven Lamps" that should light the architect's path, according to Ruskin, were those of "Sacrifice," "Truth," "Power," "Beauty," "Life," "Memory" and "Obedience." Architect of Trinity Church H.H. Richardson, like all young artists and architects of his mid- to late nineteenth-century era, would have known Ruskin's words well, both as published books and through lectures in Europe and England while Richardson studied abroad.

Historically and artistically, the towering figure, representing the meeting of art with morality, of Englishman John Ruskin hovers forever above the architecture and symbolic meaning of America's Trinity Church. From our contemporary perspective, of course, this is rather a greater ethical burden than we would ascribe to our professional designers; however, in Ruskin's philosophy, architecture was interpreted to be a kind of calling. Even Ruskin himself later in life commented, "I am sometimes accused of trying to make art too moral." What better model, however, might Richardson find for his new church in Copley Square than Ruskin's beloved St. Mark's in Venice? What better model might Richardson find as architect, aesthetic and moral thinker, than Ruskin himself? And what better place might these influences become mutually expressive than in a new, yet historically influenced, ecclesiastical house of God?

Ruskin encouraged not only to build a building well but also to ornament it with meaningful sculptural carvings and to use color symbolically—all of which would raise Boston's Trinity Church to a new level of American aesthetics. Ruskin's theories must have been inspiring for a lifetime to architect H.H. Richardson, as they remain to us today when we visit Trinity Church. In Ruskin's particularly moving words, "You must love the creation you work in the midst of."[29]

Copley Square

John La Farge, Artist

John La Farge (1835–1910), a widely talented American artist, contributed both religious-themed opalescent stained glass and historicizing painted murals to the interior décor of Trinity Church. The blue-green stained-glass figure of *Christ in Majesty* that La Farge created above the nave is the primary artistic image of the interior of Richardson's Trinity Church. The vibrant color is unique and unexpected. It casts late afternoon light into the body of the church, creating a drama beyond its own image. The flat pattern of his murals of still figures displays an appreciation for the figure delineated by line and color. At Trinity, La Farge synthesized his own Christianity with art and architecture.

A Public Form within a Public Forum

It is quite surprising, or perhaps not really so, that the professional careers and lives of the artists and architects, even the religious, of Copley Square were so intertwined. For example, architect H.H. Richardson had been a college friend of Reverend Brooks before the Trinity Church commission. Though the characters of Copley Square were individually talented professionals, they were often also the beneficiaries of lifelong, sometimes multigenerational "circles" of professional interconnections, of friends and family, in the worlds of the arts and letters—and often with connections to old money.

H.H. Richardson employed architects Charles McKim and Stanford White as draftsmen for the plans of his church, and Richardson appeared to have used drawings of Trinity Church by Stanford White, possibly incorporating White's work into the designs of Trinity Church as supporting sketches for the master's work. McKim and White, later as architect and designer of the Boston Public Library, formed their own famous partnership, McKim, Mead & White. Stanford White was also a friend of the artists of Trinity Church, including John La Farge and Augustus Saint-Gaudens. They and library muralist Puvis de Chavannes had all been students of Neo-Classical muralist Thomas Couture in Paris. If we were to chart these professional Copley relationships, so many would converge at some point in Boston and Cambridge and in Paris via European architectural and artistic travel.

Harvard University has historically been the centrum of many inspiring Boston relationships in architecture and the arts. Richardson, after Trinity Church, designed one of the most aesthetically important buildings in nineteenth-century America, Sever Hall (1880) on the Harvard University campus. Charles McKim received the commission for the gates surrounding Harvard Yard (1889). In the case of Copley Square, perhaps, circles of friends and colleagues working in collaboration have made this square aesthetically successful over time, fortunately without compromising critical judgment.

All public architecture must stand separate from its creators on its own aesthetic and ethical merits, as well as on its structural correctness. Why is this so important? Architecture, in particular, outlives its makers, so we must all live with the fruits of this art form in our urban environments, often for our lifetimes. Architecture, more than any other art, bears ethical responsibilities—for this art alone creates a lasting public form within a public forum.

Arches in American Architecture

Like classical arts and philosophy, architectural forms have endured for centuries. Consider the form and concept of the arch, both structure and ornament. The ancient Romans built stone arches, such as the Pont du Gard, throughout Europe by the first century AD; H.H. Richardson, too, used the stone arch in America in 1875. Consider one antique building all can identify from architectural history: the Roman Colosseum. It is both strong and simple, a layered building, built up of three piled rows of stone supporting arches—arches upon arches upon arches, with decorative Doric, Ionic and Corinthian Orders ascending the building (see glossary). Continuous arches create arcades and simple barrel vaults, common elements of Roman and, later, Romanesque architecture.

Let us understand Richardson's nineteenth-century style of rough stone, of columns and keystones and arches. Its often-used name "Richardsonian Romanesque" is based on the creation, first displayed in Copley Square but much copied later, of Richardson's design for Trinity Church. It has more widely come to represent a major style defining the nineteenth century in American architecture. Of course, as the name of a style, Richardsonian Romanesque is derived from the architect's name; the word Romanesque requires some historical framework.

Copley Square

A bridge in a rural Massachusetts landscape. The structural form of the arch has been transferred as design from ancient Rome to America.

The form of the arch—a strong, supporting element of stone architecture throughout history, from ancient aqueducts to modern bridges—was transferred into the provinces of Europe by the Romans, eventually integrated into the buildings of early Christians within their churches. This basic architectural form spread throughout the Roman Empire, both as structural composition and as decoration. Using the forms of the arch, the arcade and the vault, Romans constructed powerful bridges, aqueducts, arenas, basilicas and towns throughout their colonies, from Rome to France, even to England. As early Christian churches were built throughout Europe, the stone arch continued to be valued both as structural form and as decorative element. The "Roman" architecture of arches inspired, in the provinces of Europe, arched early Christian Romanesque and, eventually, pointed Gothic architecture.

In the nineteenth century, the history of the Roman, Romanesque, Gothic and Renaissance eras was respected as a full font of artistic vision and creative excellence from which the contemporary architect should draw inspiration. Long before Richardson selected the rounded arch and other

Romanesque forms of architecture for the Trinity Church competition, American churches had for decades been copying the pointed Gothic arch on their simple wooden parish churches from pattern books of details. We might see this today as a rather grab-bag usage of historical style, but it was very much respected and "au courant" in the nineteenth century to base one's current work on historical precedent.

Such creative use of artistic precedent would come to define the work of the finest nineteenth-century architects in America, including Richardson. We know that Richardson was particularly taken with the Romanesque basilica, a building type employed for law courts and early Christian churches. In addition to early Christian forms, Moorish and various other so-called exotic styles of architecture were also being discovered by European architects and by visiting Americans. Here amid these civilized constructions, Richardson found the power of the arch, the strength of rough-hewn polychrome stone and the virtues of flat-patterned ornament. These elements formed the creative inspiration and the artistic basis of his career's Romanesque oeuvre, his life's work.

CHAPTER 5

AMERICA

The Art and Architecture of Trinity Church: H.H. Richardson, Architect (circa 1875)

THE STRONG AND THE SIMPLE

It is rare for one building to engender a wholly new architectural style; it is rarer still for that building's architect alone to be the namesake of that new style, but such was the case of H.H. Richardson's Trinity Church and the inception of his Richardsonian Romanesque style. In the design of Boston's Trinity Church, Richardson displayed "a sympathetic sense of the quality of materials" and "aspired to found with Trinity an American style of architecture."[30]

We look upward to Trinity Church from Copley Square. It exudes strength, dignity, something more than that which we experience in our diurnal lives passing about this city. We stop in front of Trinity. We feel the need to be still. We may feel small and human in the face of its mass of carved stone saints and dominating towers. How does Boston's Trinity Church make this statement of more than human power via architecture and art?

Trinity engages us immediately through its intense visual and emotional presence—a powerful vertical landscape composed of masses of carved, rough-hewn blocks of colored sandstone. In this edifice, inorganic material seems to grow organically upward from ground to towers. This very original Richardsonian aesthetic style of architecture, producing in spectators strong emotional response, was best described by architectural historian Henry-Russell Hitchcock in his fundamental text, *The Architecture of H.H. Richardson* (1936), as a "taste for the strong, the simple and the rough."[31]

Trinity Church façade. The strong sandstone silhouette and the massing of architectural forms appear to transform this powerful building into a monadnock overhanging Copley Square. *Photo by K.F.K. Cormier.*

THE FORMS OF TRINITY CHURCH

Metaphorically, the form of Trinity Church is both architecture and nature. Reflecting perhaps a stone mountain, known as a New England monadnock, the church is a polychrome stone mass growing upward out of the ground below, forming contrasting cubic blocks and curvilinear arches of red and brown sandstone. The effect is here achieved through a building up of stone upon stone, a crescendo of form upon form, into an overall mass. The building is composed of, first, the solid block of the church; above that the many stone turrets; and then, high above Copley Square, the giant central tower of Trinity Church with its cross that can be seen in the sky from the square below.

"Owing to the conformation of the building—a lofty tower, with chancel, transepts, and nave running from it to the four points of the compass—the facade is not imposing, nor is there, from that view, any special evidence of the order of architecture to which it belongs. But when one has entered the doors and penetrated through the vestibule into the nave, the Moorish character is at once apparent."[32]

We note the breadth of contrasting historical allusions and eclectic use of European and "exotic" artistic forms in Richardson's Trinity Church design. High atop the church is found a Celtic-influenced cross, a circle on a Latin crucifix cross with an elongated vertical line. The ground plan of the church, however, reflects something closer to the shape of a Greek cross, with arms of equal length. In addition to the reference to the Greek cross, this author adds "Celtic" form, as well as "Venetian," to the stylistic references of Trinity Church. In the past, the words "Saracen" and "Moorish" have also been applied to this place by early critics. These complex and sometimes contradictory associations that the visitor perceives upon entering this striking church greatly enrich the aesthetic experience.

Site and Precedent in the Square

While symbolically holding a very American place in our history, Richardson's Trinity Church also follows many European traditions in its design and site placement, recalling its Medieval Christian roots. It is important to note that the placement of this American church, with its mass and façade dominating Copley Square, is set on a strong east–west axis. The site placement of the church is significant because it re-creates the ancient European cathedral tradition of placing the apse, or altar space of the church, at the east end of the building. Thus, the front portals, or entrances to cathedrals, were almost consistently found on the west end in European churches and cathedrals.

Trinity Church follows well-known European historical concepts of symmetry in plan and design. Richardson's church design, like other of his works, is "symmetrical both in plan and its front, in accordance with the École's teaching that symmetry in plan adds to ease of circulation within a building and that symmetry of elevation adds to monumentality."[33] Interestingly, Trinity Church breaks its own French École symmetry, as English cathedrals often do, by its attached Chapter House, also by Richardson.

We understand that Richardson sought to make his building historical and symbolically meaningful on many levels, influenced by myriad ecclesiastical traditions and architectural precedents of French and perhaps also English precedent. Further, the strong Anglican and English moral and aesthetic influences on art and architecture at the time of the design of Richardson's Trinity Church by the writings and lectures of Oxford Professor John Ruskin cannot be overlooked or underestimated.

In an English cathedral model, there is usually integrated landscape, an enclosed grassy open space of cathedral "green and close," directly in front of the west façade, as there is for Boston's Trinity Church—now fronting the open space of Copley Square that Richardson likely anticipated in the newly developing square. This picturesque relationship between site and building is traditionally very English. Is this relationship of church to site a clue to Richardson's design and thinking?

The siting of a cathedral with its west front and portals facing a defined flat open space, or cathedral green, is specifically English. This relationship speaks to a studied aesthetic opposition of landscape space to object of architecture, the contrast making each one more apparent to the observer. This author considers, from site visits, that the twelfth-century Anglican Wells Cathedral in Somerset, England, may have been a medieval visual precedent for Richardson's nineteenth-century design of Trinity Church, as well as its siting. Wells was one of the very earliest English Gothic churches, its style transferred to England from France at the end of the Romanesque period of rounded arches. The façade of Wells Cathedral is encrusted with carved stone arches and figures, recalling for the American viewer the simpler but similar sandstone surface of Trinity Church. Wells Cathedral may have been one British influence among many European models for Trinity Church that architects could find in travels or illustrated books, to supplement memories of the Romanesque Catholic churches of France, providing Richardson with an Anglican antecedent for an Episcopal Boston church.

Wells overlooks and defines the flat enclosed cathedral green in front, as Trinity Church now defines its open site in Copley Square. The intention of this site is even clearer today than before, due to the recent greening of our Copley Square. Both churches, Trinity in America and Wells in England, coincidentally have strong historical associations to the preexisting water under the ground on which they stand—the Charles River estuary in America and the springs of Wells in England.

The setting sun in the west dramatically strikes the façade over the green in front of Wells, due to that cathedral's east–west placement on the site, just as it does for Trinity Church in Copley Square. This means that while the dawn light rises behind these cathedrals' altars and stained glass in the morning, the sun's rays brightly light the west front doors and church steps in the late afternoon. (Though contemporary high-rise buildings block some sunlight, the sunset effects are still very present on these steps.)

Trinity Church is at once specifically religious yet open to all; impressive artistically and emotionally moving; true to stylistic and siting traditions of

French and English architectural precedents and also inventive as American style and site; historically reflective of long European artistic traditions, yet also a vital part of this contemporary city.

Inside Trinity Church

Now let us leave the bright sunlight of Copley Square and enter the inner sanctum of Richardson's landmark Trinity Church. We climb stone steps into a narrow narthex, or church entryway. We pass through heavy oak doors, walking into a wide but short nave, or central aisle of the church. Pews with needlepoint kneelers invite supplicants to pray. We adjust to the low light, and out of the afternoon darkness we emerge into a golden glowing open and uplifting space.

The word "Honour" is inscribed above, with its British spelling reminding us that this is an Anglican church. With this wording aloft above us, we recall that in the history of this church, and of Boston, Massachusetts, "Honor" has long been taken seriously, from its Revolutionary roots to its abolitionist stance. We look upward into the red and gold interior that is the cubic open space below the stone towers we first encountered outdoors.

A Building Defined by Geometry

We are in the center of Trinity Church. Now, at last, we comprehend that this building is defined by geometry: stone solids, void spaces, cruciform plan. We are walking within this geometry. As architectural historian David Van Zanten commented, "Beaux-Arts composition…was concerned with masses…with those masses as containers of space, and with those spaces as experienced when walked through."[34] The dominant logic of the building is comprehensible, though contradictory: we recall the tower and its encircling towers, yet the space does not soar into those shapes but into a cube of space floating above the other cubes of space that support it. The chancel is a semicircular dome form, completing the geometric spatial progression. We understand at last in the center of the building that we are seeing the church tower from the inside out, and like a seashell, it is chromatic and lustrously lined.

Colored Glass and Venetian Color

We feel the color. It radiates an intense aesthetic experience: red and gold, with highlights of deep blue. "Colors give a somber magnificence to the first view. Blues, greens, dull reds, and gold have been cast in scientific confusion over this ceiling and across the walls."[35] The red chosen is a particularly saturated color. It is lit by reflection and outlined in gold bands, like a medieval manuscript page. The gold motif grows to a visual crescendo behind the altar as an abstract, repetitive, flat-patterned design.

This golden wall design is the background to the most significant liturgical design, the Church's Cross. The cross of Trinity Church hangs suspended above a simplified marble altar. Note that this is not a standard cross but a cross + a circle, perhaps an ancient Celtic reference, extending other apparently Celtic motifs, such as the designs carved into the choir benches beneath the cross.

The interior decoration of Trinity is rightly considered a masterpiece of late nineteenth-century design. The most significant works are those

Campanile in the Venetian style, Old South Church, Boston.

of artist John La Farge, who created monumental figures, both in mural painting and stained glass, including his powerful window *Christ in Majesty* (1883). Within the tower, one may note the La Farge mural figures (1877) reminiscent of Michelangelo's late Renaissance Mannerist style. In stained glass, we experience the late afternoon light as it is thrown through the icy turquoise-blue opalescent glass above the west entrance.

These La Farge windows are so original, both in style and in execution, and they do not have the obvious medieval precedents of much of the other stained glass found here and in other churches. The technique of these windows, opalescent glass, is also new for its time. Indeed, La Farge's stained glass for Trinity Church became the precedent for many future stained-glass programs, particularly within the sacred spaces of New England. La Farge and Louis Comfort Tiffany remained the two major artists of opalescent glass during the late nineteenth to early twentieth century. Today, more of La Farge's work is found in the environs of Boston and more of Tiffany's in New York City and internationally.[36]

To this author, the overwhelming experience of the interior of Trinity Church, from the Venetian red and gold palette to the geometric domed space, is a haunting recall of St. Mark's Basilica, Venice, Italy. The visual and spatial memories of the play of darkness and light and of light reflected on the golden walls are strongly reminiscent of a miniaturized, but studied, Venetian effect.

A transfer of European cultural and artistic history, then, has carried a metaphorical stone from Piazza San Marco, Venice, to America, in Copley Square, Boston. One might consider that Richardson likely studied the thoughts of John Ruskin, Slade Professor of Fine Art at Oxford University, who lectured widely, and whose groundbreaking treatise *The Stones of Venice* (1851) was in print and very popular with artists and travelers, before designing Boston's Trinity Church.

Perhaps Trinity Church in Copley Square can be best appreciated by comprehending this landmark American building, with its integration of the arts with architecture, in terms of the ideals of this very influential nineteenth-century British architectural theorist, John Ruskin. Ruskin was committed to the creation of what he called "The Unity of the Fine Arts," reminding artists and architects that "Fine Art is that in which the hand, the head, and the heart of man go together."[37]

Copley Square

Architecture and Allusions

Entering Trinity Church, for this twenty-first-century American author, evokes such a multiplicity of strong visual associations with medieval St. Mark's Basilica in Venice that one can only assume that H.H. Richardson, as a European-educated nineteenth-century architect, very likely intended to recall in his structure this significant European precedent in America. He certainly would have had memories of the Venetian lagoon and canals that define that other city over water with its legendary waterways. Venice had emerged as a romantic artistic image in the mid- to late nineteenth century, leading to a new interest in the "Venetian" style in England and eventually in America. The physical site of Copley Square had a number of unusual architectural conditions in common with the very unusual site of Venice. Most striking, of course, is that both cities are built over water.

Both St. Mark's Basilica on Piazza San Marco and Trinity Church on Copley Square are enormous structures built on wooden pilings sunk into water. Each square has a major church with arches and a prominently picturesque silhouette, sited opposite more simplified rooflines around a pedestrian square. A symbol of medieval Venice was the lion, and there are a number of lion references, too, about the altar space of Trinity. Perhaps this is a small clue to unraveling Richardson's allusions to Venice.

Boston's nineteenth-century Venetian infatuation was due not only to architectural travel but also, specifically, to the writings of aesthetic theorist John Ruskin, well known at this time for his moralistic aesthetic treatise *The Seven Lamps of Architecture* (1849). Three of the "lamps" are the aesthetic concepts of "Truth," "Beauty" and "Memory." One of the most influential books on architecture of this era, and a likely choice for American architects traveling in Europe, also by Ruskin, was *The Stones of Venice*. As architectural students of the era, Richardson and the other architects of Copley Square were certain to have read and absorbed the Venetian design theory and romantic artistic symbolism. Even without travel, nineteenth-century architects would have discovered a celebration of the aesthetics of Venice via Ruskin's famous treatises, as well as in many illustrated books of the time.

It is also interesting to note that here in Boston where Richardson was building his church, he knew he was designing the first, and therefore the anchor, building for a newly created city square constructed, like Venice, over water. St. Mark's Basilica is sited dramatically on a renowned Venetian pedestrian piazza. This ancient European urban piazza form would one day be found fronting Richardson's American church as well. The use of

Venetian style is also reflected across the square in Old South Church by architects Cummings and Sears.

We see the relationship of the two churches as we look up to the Venetian campanile, or church tower, of Old South Church, standing high above the Library, opposite Trinity in Copley Square. Richardson was prescient in anticipating that the newly created crossroads of Copley Square would by the end of the nineteenth century become a significant Boston pedestrian site, as Piazza San Marco is to Venice. The architects of Copley Square created an enduring expression of ancient European influences in a newly developing American city.

CHAPTER 6

EUROPE AND AMERICA

International Designs of Cities

URBAN MODELS OF TWO MILLENNIA

For two millennia, cities have been formed by the seemingly omniscient hand of urban planning....Modern Western urban planning has its origins in the Roman concept of a coherent grid....The greatest sweep of urban planning was...to come in the deconstruction and re-assemblage of Paris in the nineteenth century. Paris saw the massive imposition of planning on a city....[Here] the grand radiating boulevards of Paris created vistas and promenade spaces through the city....

Urban planning in London is quite a contrast to Paris, for London never experienced an overlaid unifying design but remained instead a kind of crazy quilt city of interconnected sectors, some of which have within them their own individual internal order. Boston is the closest analogy to London in form: antique, irrational street patterns contrasting with 19th-century planned sectors.[38]

PARIS'S BOULEVARDS AS MODELS FOR THE BACK BAY

Paris's long, straight sightlines along boulevards, and contrasting formal squares, have made this city a particularly unique visual experience. This was not, however, always the case for this city in history. Early

Paris developed in the controlled chaos of most medieval cities: narrow, winding streets; mismatched, uneven rooflines and building setbacks; an indecipherable web of impenetrable streets and intersections. Paris is only today the place we celebrate artistically because a street plan of radiating streets, long boulevards and enclosed squares was imposed on this place by the Haussmann Plan for Paris.

These preconceived new patterns were laid down from on high in Paris via decree, design, plan and demolition. Extensive reconstruction of buildings and streets upon the ancient city in the mid-nineteenth century (1850s–'70s) by Napoleon III and his designer, Baron Haussmann, completed the famous Plan for Paris. Though we truly appreciate the fruits of Haussmann's plan today as visitors, we perhaps would not have appreciated living through the destruction of the city if we had been the inhabitants of the time. With historical irony, we note that Boston, this American city that so prided itself on revolution in the eighteenth century, by the nineteenth century would choose as its model plans imposed on a European city in such a post-revolutionary autocratic fashion. Imposition

An urban square in France, displaying the influence of ancient Rome in its Classical columns and configuration.

of plans, destruction and construction create a serious conundrum for urban planning in every country and every era.

Yet this transformative artistic plan for architecture and landscape re-created the ancient European city into the modern and visually sophisticated Paris we celebrate today—as well as its American derivative, architect Arthur Gilman's mid-nineteenth-century plans for Boston's Back Bay (1860s) and Copley Square. An extreme form of urban design and construction had been effective in Paris, greatly appreciated as one of history's superior city designs. As we walk today toward Copley Square, from the Boston Common, through the Public Garden, along Back Bay's Commonwealth Avenue, we admire the promenade, the processional space, the treed mall. We recall while we walk there and back that these American spaces resulted from the aesthetic advances of nineteenth-century French urban design. History, and our walk today, culminates in the dramatic light and visual climax of Copley Square.

As we explore the enclosed sense of open space of Copley Square, we become aware of the overarching architectural relationships that form this urban place into an almost operatic aesthetic experience. There are themes that play together, and in counterpoint, in this space. There are major works of architecture, and each has an echo within the space. Trinity Church with its interior Venetian form is echoed across Copley Square in Old South Church. The Boston Public Library is echoed in the Beaux-Arts architecture of the Copley Plaza Hotel. The tall, attenuated form of the Hancock Tower is a modern echo of the campanile of Old South Church. Most significantly, the dramatic picturesque silhouette of Trinity Church is played in counterpoint to the regularity of the cornice and the rhythmic repetition of forms of the Boston Public Library.

London's Squares as Models for Copley Square

Covent Garden is the originator of London's, and subsequently of Boston's, distinctive patterns of enclosed pedestrian squares. This model of urban development creates an oasis of open pedestrian space within the city. Covent Garden "piazza" is an Italian-derived invention of "the square" as city form that would become a precedent for Boston's Louisburg Square and later for Copley Square. Interestingly, Covent Garden, like Copley Square, was developed to enhance and to enclose an urban square anchored by a church: in London, St. Paul's Church; in Boston, Trinity Church.

Designed by the seminal seventeenth-century British architect Inigo Jones, "Covent" referred to the square as the early site of a "convent" and its garden, later to become a speculative residential development. The seventeenth-century Italian piazza form became the eighteenth-century British residential and commercial urban place, a common urban design form in London and outside the city. Still in use throughout Britain, urban squares are found as form in the Bloomsbury sector of London, in Russell Square, Bedford Square and Tavistock Square, as well as in the cities of Bristol and Bath.

This transported Italian to British to American urban design form became the model for the extensive eighteenth- and nineteenth-century development of squares in Bloomsbury and Mayfair, some of the most beautiful sectors of London, even today. This ancient model was later exported to America, as noted, in the creation of Louisburg Square on Boston's Beacon Hill, a place that eventually itself became an eighteenth-century domestic scale model for the much larger and more active

Covent Garden, London, by architect Inigo Jones, originator of London's squares as urban form.

History through Architecture

Tavistock Square, Bloomsbury, London.

Louisburg Square, Beacon Hill, Boston.

nineteenth-century urban form of Copley Square. "Louisburg Square is an elegant residential enclave of great charm and character. It was planned by the Mt Vernon Proprietors in 1820.…The Greek Revival and Late Federal houses…reminiscent of Regency Brighton and Bath [England], make the old square one of the places which most poignantly recalls the English heritage of Old Boston."[39]

What differentiates the early London and Louisburg squares from the later Copley Square, however, is that while the early squares could concentrate only on pedestrian space, Copley Square has always had to contend with extensive moving vehicular and trolley traffic. Both London's squares and Boston's Louisburg Square are lined by striking black wrought-iron fences and gates, separating the square from the street while defining shape and periphery. Copley Square, by necessity, must integrate its space into the surrounding urban motion. In all these urban places, the central fixture of the "square" is the rectangle of protected green pedestrian space in the center. Comparing Louisburg Square, Boston, to Russell Square, London, a historian wrote of "its retired charm and English flavor," for in Louisburg Square is found "an environment sufficiently English in its qualities to satisfy the needs of the occasion."[40]

Urban Design in American Cities

Here in one American city, Boston, a London square is found amid Parisian boulevards, as we have seen. Architecturally, here in Copley Square, a French Romanesque façade faces an Italian Renaissance design, and as the cover of this book illustrates, the Modernism of the American skyscraper reflects, quite literally, old-world architecture. Pieces of all these European urban models have over time coalesced today into Boston as we know it.

It is interesting to note that since the earliest colonial days, Boston generally chose not to follow the formal principles of urban design that were imposed on other major American cities. Boston's early layout involved a seventeenth-century open "Common" or public green pasture, as the name implies, a public and enclosed open space configuration of New England settlements. Many irrational meandering streets shaped the early city; only the development on Beacon Hill was basically rational in the seventeenth and eighteenth centuries, before the nineteenth-century planning of the Back Bay.

History through Architecture

Commonwealth Avenue in Boston's Back Bay, a short walk from Copley Square. The influence of Parisian boulevards is felt in this pedestrian promenade toward the Public Garden.

Many American cities were experiencing intense growth between the late eighteenth to late nineteenth centuries. A century of American urbanization based on population growth, industrialization and European immigration created rapidly expanding American cities. Facing similar urban demand for growth, American cities found varying design solutions. Let us briefly compare Boston's contemporaries, including New York City; Washington, D.C.; and San Francisco.

Grid, Vista and Beaux-Arts Cities in America

The urban designs of New York City, with its planned checkerboard street grid, and Washington, D.C., with its planned vistas, are reflected only in selected sectors in Boston. Developing near in time but far away in space, nineteenth-century San Francisco may be the closest major American parallel in urban planning history to Boston.

Boston eschewed the commercial design plan for New York City: the urban grid. New York City, as early as 1811, had laid out the grid of intersecting avenues and streets on paper. From Wall Street in lower Manhattan, northward throughout Manhattan Island, from the East River to the Hudson River, New York City was planned. Fortunately, Central Park was later introduced into the grid, before it was too late to save the open space—a lesson for all developing cities.

Though there are neighborhoods of separately gridded streets in Boston, including Beacon Hill and the Back Bay, this is not the dominant form of this city. Most of Boston is not consciously arranged in grids. Among the unevenly gridded streets of eighteenth-century Beacon Hill, for example, Louisburg Square is surely the most significant consciously designed urban form, based on the London square. The closest pattern in Boston to a grid is found in the nineteenth-century avenues and cross streets of the Back Bay and in the previous similar grid in the South End. The Boston grids, however, do not impose the strong city blocks that New York does; rather, in Boston, they emphasize the promenade effects of their primary avenues, such as Boston's Commonwealth Avenue in the Back Bay and Boylston Street along Copley Square.

A century apart, Boston's Back Bay, like Washington, D.C., before it, selected French-influenced design for the construction of long boulevards with urban views and vistas toward dramatic sites in its city planning. The walk along the Champs-Élysées toward the climactic Arc de Triomphe still amazes the visiting pedestrian today in Paris. A French-influenced vista can be seen today as one walks along the Mall in Washington, D.C., or along Boston's Commonwealth Avenue toward the somewhat less but still dramatic site of the Public Garden. Haussmann's plan for Paris was strongly influential both for Washington, D.C., and the Back Bay, in the vistas created by their Beaux-Arts city designs.

European influences are very apparent in Boston and Washington, D.C., for French architect L'Enfant designed Washington, D.C., and French-educated American architect Arthur Gilman designed Boston's Back Bay. "Gilman was responsible for the Back Bay's street layout, considered the first such French Academic design in America."[41] Though this vision of imposed urban planning was quite extreme at the time in a preexisting historical city such as Haussmann's Paris, it made real sense in a wholly new city, such as in the case of Washington, or on land newly created, in Boston. The United States capital and the Back Bay of Boston are Beaux-Arts places of promenades and vistas built in former swamps on land newly created specifically for these plans. San Francisco was unintentionally cleared for planning by the 1906 earthquake and fire.

History through Architecture

Urban Squares and Beaux-Arts Architecture

The closest major American city, visually and developmentally, to Boston, Massachusetts, in the opinion of this author, is San Francisco, California. Though these cities are found three thousand miles apart, on the Atlantic and the Pacific Oceans, they share many analogous physical characteristics. Their topography was naturally similar, though as we have seen, Boston's natural geological forms have been much changed. Though both harbors were once surrounded by hills, now only San Francisco retains its hilly forms. The histories of Boston and San Francisco strongly reflect their coastal sites: cities on ocean harbors, reached once only by long sailing ship passages, active in trade and once in the transit of émigrés—Boston for the colonies, San Francisco for the gold rush.

The layout and design of both Boston and San Francisco have sectors that were laid out in grids, as well as Beaux-Arts sectors and architecture. Both display significant public architecture within Beaux-Arts squares. San Francisco's Union Square and the city's Civic Center are analogous spaces

Repetition of the row house type on Beacon Hill, arranged around a city square. This American urban form is based on London's architecture.

to Boston's Copley Square. These are renowned landmarks and central public meeting places in the midst of urban grids. Each of the grids of these two cities displays one unusual characteristic: these cities were built with two different urban grids meeting at acute angles, creating major diagonal streets. Boston's Huntington Avenue and San Francisco's Market Street are found between those grids, and each street has become a major urban thoroughfare. Near these major grids and streets are found two of the most interesting pedestrian squares in America: Boston's Copley Square and San Francisco's Union Square.

The clearest analogy between Boston and San Francisco is visual and stylistic—both these American cities were strongly European influenced by nineteenth-century French Beaux-Arts architecture and urban design. The Beaux-Arts style of the Boston Public Library, the primary precedent for urban public libraries in America, became the style, and likely an American architectural model (though both are based on French precedent), for the San Francisco Public Library. The design of Copley Square's nineteenth-century European-influenced architecture, the Boston Public Library, crossed the American continent to the West Coast to influence the design of the San Francisco Public Library (1917) by the early twentieth century. It is interesting to note that the original building of the San Francisco Public Library has now become the home of the Asian Art Museum of San Francisco.

Thus, a cultural circle has been completed: the Beaux-Arts style has crossed the Atlantic to America and then traversed the continent to the Pacific. Completing its influence as cultural icon, the Beaux-Arts style has now been transferred via nineteenth-century city design and public architecture from European style in Paris, to American form in Boston, to a wholly new twentieth-century Asian context in San Francisco.

Urban Parks in American Cities

Boston's own seventeenth- and eighteenth-century public pasture, the Boston Common, and nineteenth-century landscaped Public Garden were early precedents for the creation and protection of open spaces within cities, and as such, they are meaningful historical symbols pointing the way toward public urban open space as created in Copley Square. At first just a crossroads within the developing Back Bay, Copley Square has now at

Nature within the city. A view of Central Park, New York City, designed by Frederick Law Olmsted and Calvert Vaux. *Photo by P.F. Powell.*

last reached its potential as an urban open space of parklike green amid architecture of stone. As the United States urbanized in the nineteenth century, some growing cities wisely agreed that open space and parklands for the public should be set aside within the urban fabric—before all land was developed.

A major movement in public urban parks ensued in cities, best seen in the work of Frederick Law Olmsted and Calvert Vaux in their Greensward Plan (1858) for the creation of New York City's Central Park, a major American urban undertaking of international fame. It was for its time, and for all time, a world-class feat of landscape design and civil engineering. Over 750 acres of rocky landscape were carved into a "naturalistic" environment—more natural than nature, with picturesque viewpoints for urban pedestrians. The theatrical illusion of untouched nature within a giant city was effected via wandering paths amid trees, lakes, fields and sunken crossroads, Roman-like bridges and overpasses and the hidden trails of the naturalistic Ramble. Yet above this nature, today we see the city's skyscrapers.

New York's Central Park and Boston's Copley Square together prove that we can create the illusion and engineer our "natural" landscape to be more "natural" than nature, even while the trees and grass are surrounded on all sides by tall buildings. Early American urban parks, including Copley, demonstrate that humans respond to sensitive design of open space within the confines of the city. We can integrate trees into our stone cities humanely. Thus, nature is both contained and celebrated within the geometry of the city.

Contemplating a Copley Canal

Would it not have been impressive if Boston had completed the nineteenth-century's Venetian imagery and had, with historical reference, designed Copley Square as our own Grand Canal? Instead of underground trolleys in the Back Bay, today we would have gondolas. But alas, the water under the Back Bay of Boston is contained, and as far as this author is aware, no such feature has ever been considered.

The European image in America would be complete with a Copley Canal (and a bit outlandish, perhaps). A romantic vision of Venice, imported during an era of nineteenth-century architectural nostalgia remains still, however, for us in the twenty-first century, to imagine, here in Copley Square, in a Venetian fog of historical associations. Ruskin's concepts of "Truth" and "Beauty" could be transported into this square of a contemporary American city, built on the recall of European architectural precedent, or "Memory,"[42] of the forms of cities of the past. Envision a Copley Canal.

CHAPTER 7

AMERICA

The National Significance of the Boston Public Library

The Public Library of The City of Boston Built by The People and Dedicated to the Advancement of Learning…
—*the inscription on the entablature of the Boston Public Library, atop the façade overlooking Copley Square*

It is impossible to overstate the significance of the Boston Public Library to the intellectual and social history of the United States, for here is first found our public access to the continuity of Classical thought within America. This was the first place in which the concept of "library" as we know it today was invented. Founded in 1852, first opened to the public in 1854, this is the first institution in America to meld the concepts of scholarly research with general enjoyment in reading and to share books fully, and freely, with the public. "The Library was previously sited on Boylston Street near the Boston Common. In 1895, with expansion, it was removed to its present location in Copley Square."[43]

This edifice and its collection represent not only an expansion of a building type in America but also, more importantly, a democratic expansion of the intellectual sharing of cultural resources with the public. It was, in particular, a breaking of class barriers to educational access for all. "Boston Public Library is the pioneer of free municipal libraries in any American city… based on far-sighted principles of public education."[44]

Boston has long defined itself as the "Athens of America." This distinction may be true, based on Boston's very early understanding of how education

Science, companion sculpture to Art, in front of the Boston Public Library.

and reading share and protect the classical ideals and American rights for all. In the opinion of this writer, this building will forever represent an American innovative intellectual equation: Books + Architecture = American Freedom of Thought.

A Classical Education for Everyman and Its Expression in Architectural Form

Reading the names of the famous thinkers chiseled on the front façade of the Boston Public Library, facing Copley Square, is an invitation to a Classical education available inside. Engraved on the walls are the names of famous philosophers, artists, humanists and scientists of the past, from Aristotle and Plato, to Michelangelo and Raphael, to Newton and Einstein, to Socrates and Leonardo da Vinci—every name and philosophy that a humanist education might explore. The two seated figures in front of the entrance, emotive and beautiful black iron sculptures of 1912,[45] beneath the famous names inscribed above them, embody the Classical spirits of Ars et Scientia, or Arts and Sciences.

The Boston Public Library is significant historically for all three of the words in its title: "Boston," as a prime colonial and Revolutionary city; "Public," for the innovative concept of the Public Good as expressed through books; and "Library," in the integration of the scholarly research collection with the new idea of the everyday lending library. Not surprisingly, it was Benjamin Franklin who had first proposed the concept of the lending library. Previously, libraries in America had been either private book collections of the wealthy or paid subscription institutions to the public. Today, the Boston Public Library serves the city's population of over half a million people. There are antique archives but also this year's best-selling books to borrow. The circulating collection is housed in its recently renovated modern Johnson Building.

The "BPL" is a welcoming place. Yes, you can walk in—and yes, it is free! The Boston Public Library truly is the People's Palace. The Boston Public Library was named a National Historical Landmark in 1987.

Special Collections and Archives of the Boston Public Library

The library serves scholars and history itself via its Special Collections, including Rare Books and Manuscripts; Prints and Drawings; and Fine Arts Department, all appropriately housed in the historical Beaux-Arts McKim Building.[46] To comprehend the wealth of American civilization for which the Boston Public Library is the trusted keeper, let us explore very briefly a few of its archival collections, this but a small selection of rare documents in the library's archives, from the seventeenth to the twentieth century:

Colonial-Era Collections
The Bay Psalm Book
Works of Increase and Cotton Mather (John A. Lewis Library of Americana)

Revolutionary War–Era Collections
Collection of Washingtonia (George Washington's farewell address) (Walter Updike Lewisson)
Massachusetts Lafayette Association Archives
Benjamin Franklin (1706–1790) Collection

Maps and Maritime Collections
History of the Port of Boston (Lane/Mead Boston Maritime Collection)
Norman B. Leventhal Center Map Collection

Civil War–Era Collections
Antislavery manuscripts
Emancipation Proclamation (Abraham Lincoln) (Civil War Papers)

Nineteenth-Century Copley Square Collections
Architectural competition drawings for the McKim Building of the Boston Public Library (1880s)
John Ruskin correspondence (1880s)

Nineteenth- and Twentieth-Century Social Issues Collections
Seaman's Orphan and Children's Friend Society, Salem (Massachusetts Charitable Societies Records)
Lewis Hine Prints (1930s, child labor in New England)

Selected American and European Architects, Artists and Designers of the Boston Public Library

Charles Follen McKim, Architect of McKim, Mead & White

American cities would be very different places without the contributions of Charles Follen McKim (1847–1909)—more mundane, less meaningful and less architecturally aspirational urban places. It is likely that without McKim's balance of the sophisticated and the rational with the humane, urban architecture in America would have yielded to the extremes of either commerce or visual Victorianism. Instead, his education at L'École des Beaux-Arts in Paris, as well as his European architectural travel, flavored his sophisticated future American works in Boston, Providence, Newport and New York. Charles Follen McKim was awarded the Gold Medal of the American Institute of Architects in 1909.

McKim, of abolitionist stock, put his efforts and his money behind his empathy for the less fortunate, as well as for students of his atelier, or studio. He followed the values he had learned early, particularly evident in his endowing architectural fellowships at the American Academy in Rome for Americans in Europe.[47] This thoughtful generosity illustrates that McKim was an excellent choice for the design of the Boston Public Library; he consistently stood for the importance of intellectual history, as well as for contemporary public enlightenment.

McKim must have been a generous and natural teacher. Attesting to his creativity and character are the successes of students of his atelier and his office: Carrere and Hastings, architects of the New York Public Library; Cass Gilbert, architect of the Woolworth Building, New York; and John Russell Pope, architect of the Frick Art Reference Library, New York.[48] As previously noted, McKim had begun his career as a draftsman for H.H. Richardson, architect of Trinity Church. As Richardson had been impressed by the Romanesque style of the ninth and tenth centuries, McKim, in particular, would personally find inspiration in the Italian Renaissance of the fifteenth and sixteenth centuries.

McKim did not work only on major public buildings in the French Beaux-Arts style; he also advanced a modernized wooden shingled version of American Colonial Revival architecture for comfortable country venues. The Newport Casino (1880), now the International Tennis Hall of Fame in Newport, Rhode Island, is an excellent example of this more informal style of McKim.

Throughout his life, McKim displayed his interests in both European and American historical design that advanced the architecture of the United States in the nineteenth and early twentieth centuries. Charles Follen McKim lived his beliefs. Later in life, he underscored his commitment to the Classical Renaissance visions of architecture and to the humanist values of antiquity. Even as McKim looked to the past for form, he also looked ahead, for the benefit of future students of architecture, as a founder of the American Academy in Rome. It is fitting that he received the gold medal of both the American Institute of Architects in 1909 and of the Royal Institute of British Architects in 1903, acknowledged on both sides of the Atlantic.

In addition to the Boston Public Library, readers may also wish to visit these architectural sites in New England by McKim, Mead & White: the Rhode Island State Capitol, Providence, Rhode Island; the Newport Casino, Newport, Rhode Island; and Naumkeag Estate, Stockbridge, Massachusetts.

Stanford White, Designer

One of the most creative artists, architectural draftsmen and interior designers in American history, Stanford White (1853–1906) displayed in his work the sophisticated interests in European design that advanced American architecture in the nineteenth and early twentieth centuries, providing the visual finesse to the interiors of the firm of McKim, Mead & White that would set it apart among Early Modern firms.

   White's draftsmanship and creativity were found both in early drawings for Richardson's Trinity Church and in his most important work, in his partnership for the Boston Public Library. Stanford White traveled and studied within Europe, honing his creative design innovations that can be found from New York to Boston to Newport, from church to library to country houses. Architect and bon vivant to the end, Stanford White was killed in a love triangle, dying tragically after an evening at the original Madison Square Garden, in a building of his own firm's design.

Pierre Puvis de Chavannes, Muralist

Although the murals above the marble staircase of McKim's Boston Public Library are in truth painted on canvas, they appear to be flat frescos adhering directly to the walls, as in an Italian palazzo. Puvis de Chavannes (1824–1898) actually painted these long murals specifically for the library while at his studio in Paris and shipped them to Boston. Puvis was an excellent choice for the Boston Public Library artistically and symbolically, for his work showed qualities that this library would share with other European institutions.

   Puvis had previously designed murals for the Sorbonne, the Universite de Paris and the Pantheon in Paris, representing concepts such as Knowledge, Truth, great personages and human ideals. Puvis de Chavannes painted the Classical and allegorical murals above the entrance stairways of the Boston Public Library. A cross-cultural influence may be visible in an ironic way in the murals: there is a curious panel above the stair that appears to juxtapose an Italian Renaissance angel with a modern American electric light pole.

John Singer Sargent, Painter

John Singer Sargent (1856–1925) is without doubt one of the greatest American painters, and he, too, was educated and traveled widely in Europe. American by citizenship, Sargent grew up in Italy and France, and this European flavor was always visible in his American work. His mural cycle for the Boston Public Library is particularly dark in color and meaning, with strong religious commentary. It is a difficult work to view, both for its placement and its meaning, a kind of conundrum to comprehend, but effort to find and observe this work will be rewarding. Anyone with a wider interest in nineteenth-century painting will want to visit the Boston Museum of Fine Arts to see, in particular, among Sargent's paintings, the canvas of *The Daughters of Edward Darley Boit*, painted in Paris (1882).

Augustus and Louis Saint-Gaudens, Sculptors

Notable among the artists to be commissioned for the decoration of the Boston Public Library were the Saint-Gaudens brothers, friends of architect Charles McKim. Together, they contributed in their careers some of the most moving public sculpture in Boston or any American city, with strong commentary on the tragedies of war.

Augustus Saint-Gaudens (1848–1907) was particularly renowned as the artist of the abolitionist Robert Gould Shaw Memorial Fifty-Fourth Regiment of the Civil War (1897) on Beacon Hill, a bronze bas-relief that can be seen near the Massachusetts State House. Augustus also contributed

Mural of Classical philosophers in the Library.

to Boston his designs for exterior motifs of the library. His brother Louis Saint-Gaudens (1854–1913) conveyed another meaningful statement on the tragedies of war via the marble lions that forever sleep symbolically in the vestibule of the Boston Public Library.

CHAPTER 8

EUROPE AND AMERICA

The Architecture and Art of the Boston Public Library: McKim, Mead & White, Architects (1895)

Architecture as Acropolis

The Boston Public Library is an archive of Western Civilization within a civilized building. This library is certainly among the most socially and aesthetically meaningful constructions and works of art in the United States. It represents the coming together of an urbane sense of European with American art and architectural design, with education, history, civics, engineering and symbolic significance.

The Boston Public Library is a conscious recall of the Renaissance, just as the Renaissance itself was a conscious memory of antiquity. Here in this American building, a latter-day Renaissance palazzo, or urban palace, has again taken form, not for royalty or the privileged class but, instead, for the American public. Through layers of architectural precedent and the transfer of European forms, the intellectual and artistic threads of Western history and culture here have been carried from the antiquity of Athens and Rome, to the Renaissance of Rome and Florence, to Paris via the historical precedents of the Beaux-Arts style, on to modern Boston.

This building displays the rich visual associations and unchanging forms—the accretions of history—as only the art of architecture can fully present to us. A review of some of the accolades this building and its architect, Charles Follen McKim, have received from major critics and architectural theorists over a century of commentary attests to its aesthetic and social significance.

The Boston Public Library. Note the simplicity and grace of the Beaux-Arts Renaissance palazzo façade, with arched windows, ironwork and sculpture.

The *New York Times* art critic called it, upon its opening in 1885, "one of the Handsomest Buildings in the United States," reviewing it as "the magnificent new library...generally acknowledged to be one of the half dozen structures on this continent that are pre-eminently grand in conception and execution," and writing that "it has a very commanding site in Copley Square, in the heart of the Back Bay, which contains as large a proportion of the fine structures in modern Athens as the Acropolis did in the ancient Athens."[49]

As architectural historian Leland Roth has stated, "The work of McKim, Mead & White [displayed] classical formality...part of the rich European architectural tradition to which the United States considered itself heir... now embellished with the collaborative work of painters and sculptures.... They sought a new 'Renaissance' or at least a resurgence of the variant Renaissance carried across the Atlantic."[50]

Architectural historian and theorist William H. Jordy commented, "The balance and clarity of the elevation of the Boston Public Library as a whole...complements the elegance and precision of the detail, to result in a façade which is certainly unsurpassed." Jordy further noted, "For McKim, Beauty was, if not precisely the starting point, at least his motto for design."[51]

Facing the Square: Façade and Elevation of the Boston Public Library

In the late nineteenth and early twentieth centuries, bringing European imagery to America was considered to be the height of correctness in architecture. The Classical ancients were respected as the finest models for modern people. One need look no further than the front façade of McKim's library itself to confirm this intellectual interest in the copying of the ancients in the arts, humanities and even sciences.

Like a Renaissance palazzo, the front is composed of layers, appropriately advancing from street to roofline. Our eyes move upward from the street-level formal front steps, to the "rusticato," or rusticated rougher stone entrance level, to the lighter upper story with arched windows. A rhythmic, almost

Copley Square as public space, defined and refined by the Renaissance façade and pedestrian stairs leading to the Boston Public Library.

"The exterior elevation facing Copley Square is 225 feet long and 70 feet high from sidewalk to cornice....It follows the general divisions of a Renaissance palazzo." (Wick quotation on the library; Old South Church seen above). *Photo by K.F.K. Cormier.*

"musical" row of repeating arches graces this façade, and three dramatic central door arches echo the windows in the main entrance below. This portal is articulated with three sets of heavy decorative bronze doors and strong black curvilinear wrought-iron lamps.

This building "stands broad, low, and white, on its graceful platform of granite, each block supporting those above it lightly and firmly, and decorated with ornaments so fine and fitting it seems perfectly harmonious throughout....Directly beneath the eaves is the inscription, which reaches across the entire front of the building: The Public Library of the City of Boston—Built By the People and Dedicated to the Advancement of Learning."[52]

The simplified rectangular front façade facing Copley Square, with its rows of arches and windows within the flat granite wall, is rhythmic—almost musical. Its façade is simple, clean, flat, punctuated only by rhythmic lines of arched windows and entry. This is a deceptively simple building from the street; like a Renaissance palace, it turns its quiet screened front to the street, consciously concealing the opulent life inside. The Boston Public Library is a stylized and graceful jewel box, holding inside the books and archives and manuscripts that represent a civilization. "The six bronze doors…are the work of sculptor Daniel Chester French with allegorical figures arranged in pairs: Music and Poetry (left), Knowledge and Wisdom (center), and Truth and Romance (right)."[53]

Inside the Boston Public Library

Against the flatness of the library façade, flanking the entrance gates, sit two entrancing figures in sweeping black robes: Ars et Scientia, or Arts and Sciences, the very core of all Western thought held in trust between them, within this library. These two highly dramatized figures enrich the portals in counterpoint to the flat façade. They are indeed powerful symbols. It is clear to this author that the sculptor, Bela Pratt, was inspired by Michelangelo's figures, including his emotive Renaissance sculpture in the Medici tombs in Florence.

Surprisingly, this expressive figure pair was not added to the library façade until 1912. It is now difficult to imagine the library entrance without them. Their black robes give real majesty to this façade. They enframe the triple iron doors and complete the wrought-iron design motifs of the unusual lamp stanchions and the formal black iron gates. They seem to honor and to protect the Classical ancestors who created the intellectual world we have here inherited. Arts and Sciences, seated here, personified, overwhelm us, at once threatening, dramatic and sublimely beautiful. Between these powerful figures, we are drawn into the library's portals, to know this building, this People's Palace, and its intellectual treasures within. Here we enter the world of ideas.

Copley Square

The Arts in Processional Spaces

From the controlled and urbane façade of the library on Copley Square, we now enter the rich and sensuous marble domed and arcuated, or arched, interiors of the Boston Public Library. Beaux-Arts architecture is never static but, rather, an experience of spatial flow. Processional design draws the visitor onward, through the space and toward a sculpture, an artwork or an open room. Like music, Beaux-Arts architecture rhythmically builds toward crescendo. The Boston Public Library is the perfect illustration of the concept of the philosopher Goethe, who stated, "Architecture is frozen music."

Two graceful, silent, *couchant* or sleeping marble lions, by sculptor Louis Saint-Gaudens, guard the interior entrance and the main staircase into the library. One might ask: Is this symbol ironic? Would sleeping lions actually make good guardians? The answer lies deeper in the nineteenth-century use of symbolism. Lions have represented strength and leadership and have been revered guardians throughout history—from ancient Rome to Venice

Lions in the vestibule of the Boston Public Library. Processional spaces that dramatically advance, via a sequence of rooms, stairs and vistas, are a significant part of the experience of the Beaux-Arts.

to Boston. Here, however, they are tributes to long-dead Civil War regiments whose men, too, remain "couchant" in peace.

Beyond these lions, the single marble staircase divides in two, ascending to the books and other works of art. Thus, we are drawn immediately upward toward the Bates Reading Room, the primary public space of this public palace of thought and contemplation. Along the stair, itself a journey in polychrome marble, moving either up or down, we encounter some of the ideas we seek. On the stairway walls, Classical thought itself is personified by allegorical figures of Philosophy and Arts, with their frozen ancient Greek dress and stylized gestures. A mural cycle, entitled *The Muses*, by artist Puvis de Chavannes, depicts Art in its antique inception.

Today, the arts of the Boston Public Library explore for us the integration of ideas and ideals, of human meaning, of the continuity of the past with the present. Perhaps today we are less high-minded, more specialized, less appreciative of "appropriate form." These deeply felt and poignant paintings, however, remind us that what unites contemporary life with human history is the search for meaning—often found in the questions of philosophy and the beauty of the arts. These murals go to the very concept of this important landmark library.

On the meaning and significance of the symbolic decorative programs of the two primary edifices of Copley Square, the Boston Public Library and Trinity Church, architectural historian William H. Jordy concluded, "These are the highpoints in McKim's attempt to recreate the Renaissance union of the arts. Richardson had earlier attempted the same in Trinity."[54]

A Library, Architectural Precedent and L'École in America

For more than a century, life in Copley Square has moved along, through peace and wars, summers and winters, while the McKim building sits sphinxlike in stone, silent and enduring, unchanged by changing street configurations outside or trolleys below—a lasting landmark to Boston and to civilization. The meaning of "Palace for the People" is well documented by McKim's symbolic and physical form in his use of the precedent of the Italian Renaissance palazzo form for the façade of the Boston Public Library.

McKim and White had both traveled extensively in Europe, and this shows well in their library. Both studied the use of ancient precedent in their designs at the École des Beaux-Arts in Paris. At the École, American students became fluent in the history and theory of architecture, from the antiquity of Greece and Rome, to French Romanesque and Gothic churches, to Roman bridges and Florentine Renaissance palaces. From these works, they learned to select specific precedents or historical buildings and forms to use as inspirations and models for their own architecture. McKim and White's grasp of European architecture was particularly insightful and detailed, and their drawings and sketches were subtle and insightful.

The success of this American library is directly attributable to its architects' French Beaux-Arts education. Charles Follen McKim and Stanford White had traveled as architecture students, studying and sketching the historical buildings of Europe and the ancient world. This education taught them to value architectural precedent highly. One searched for the appropriate form for a library. One then used that precedent not only for plan, layout and design of the building but simultaneously comprehended and respected the historical precedent as a high aesthetic standard to be emulated in one's own architecture. Their great respect for the historical precedents of European architecture demanded that their own contemporary Boston Public Library exceed and set a new aesthetic standard for American public works.

The formal and functional design of the Boston Public Library was inspired by the two iconic Beaux-Arts libraries of Paris, La Bibliotheque (Library) Sainte-Genevieve and the original building of La Bibliotheque Nationale, both designed by French architect Henri Labrouste (1801–1875). Labrouste's influence was spread via L'École des Beaux-Arts in Paris, where generations of American architects studied, to Boston. "The success of the French academic system appeared impressive and exemplary. Foreign architectural students were attracted to the school in great numbers and returned home to create local varieties of Beaux-Arts curricula. There… came into being the idea that there existed a single, all-encompassing Beaux-Arts system."[55]

The Courtyard of the Boston Public Library

After winning the commission for the Boston Public Library, the designers of McKim, Mead & White drew heavily on Italian Renaissance motifs, as interpreted through the French Beaux-Arts style of the day. It should be remembered that the meaning of "Renaissance" itself implies the use of precedent, the "rebirth" of Classical antiquity, so we see that architecture has always sought models for designs of the current times in the works of the past. For his design of the Copley Square façade and the interior courtyard, McKim clearly studied Italian Renaissance precedents. The influence of the palazzo style is very clear in the façade of the building, as previously discussed, but the design and its precedent for the interior courtyard deserves further consideration, as well.

For the façade, McKim looked for inspiration to the prevalent image of the Renaissance palazzo, as found in Rome and Florence, continued as a form in Paris. Any number of the many historically significant public buildings of Italy and France were excellent architectural models for McKim as he studied architecture at the École des Beaux-Arts in Paris. Even the Palais

The central Courtyard with fountain in the Boston Public Library, one of the finest public spaces in America. The columns and arches are references to the architecture of the Italian Renaissance. *Photo by K.F.K. Cormier.*

des Etudes de L'École des Beaux-Arts, or the academic building of his own architectural school, would have been influential to the young McKim.

Most significant for the front façade facing Copley Square of the Boston Public Library for McKim, though, was La Bibliotheque Sainte-Genevieve (1850s), a major historical archive and library of Paris. This building was a public work by the innovative architect and structural designer Henri Labrouste (1801–1875) and a strong visual influence on McKim's façade design of the Boston Public Library, in the view of this and other historians.

For the interior open outdoor Courtyard of the Boston Public Library, however, McKim apparently found a different precedent. Here he re-created a romantic revival of an Italian Renaissance piazza with a fountain within Copley Square. The question arises as to what was his specific artistic influence? At which historical precedent from the Renaissance was McKim looking? It has often been written that the model for the elegant Courtyard of the Boston Public Library is considered to be the High Renaissance Palazzo della Cancelleria (1495), a property of the Vatican in Rome. Yet might there be a meaningful earlier Italian architectural precedent for this Boston courtyard?

Finding Florence in Copley Square

There may be an even more significant architectural precedent to consider. At the time of construction of our Boston library, one erudite art critic of the *New York Times* specifically pointed to "the stately beauty of the Florentine school" (emphasis on the word "Florentine") that he had observed at the Boston Public Library.[56]

The author of this book suggests that the true precedent for Boston's Beaux-Arts Library Courtyard is the earlier Florentine Ospedale degli Innocenti (1419), or Home of the Innocents, or Orphanage for Children. This beautiful building on a sunny piazza was the work of one of the most important artist-architects of the Florentine Early Renaissance, Filippo Brunelleschi (1377–1446). The graceful linear clarity of this design, the lightness of the single story of arches, the decorative orders of the columns and the arrangement of the round medallions we find at the Boston Public Library all appear directly referential to Brunelleschi's graceful and linear Florentine Early Renaissance style.

History through Architecture

 This historical visual distinction, of Roman versus Florentine style, would have been very clear to architects of the nineteenth-century Beaux-Arts, who were fully imbued with the knowledge and forms of the Renaissance. Architect Charles McKim was astute and discerning in his knowledge of Italian Renaissance precedents—so much so that he later became a benefactor of the American Academy in Rome. One can only conclude that naming a later Roman edifice, the Cancelleria, as model for the Boston Public Library could unlikely be an aesthetic oversight of this architect.

Therefore, it might be considered in the manner of the nineteenth century that it perhaps was deemed more "appropriate" to name the Cancelleria (a palace) rather than the Innocenti (an orphanage) as the historical inspiration for this American library courtyard. Though the library was to be considered the People's Palace, it seems that perhaps it was sought to give a lineage of a higher class to this design. Thus, this author submits, rather ruefully, that the prevalent class system of late nineteenth-century America may have dictated that the new Boston Public Library would be better to claim the prestige of a Roman palazzo design than to be known to recall in form a Florentine orphanage for the poor.

Perhaps we can today more generously and insightfully appreciate the influence of Brunelleschi's gracefully humane design for a Florentine

Veduta, or view, of Florence, Italy, showing Florentine Renaissance architecture. *Unsigned etching, collection of the author.*

orphanage on our own Boston Public Library Courtyard in Copley Square, finally finding Florence in Copley Square. Architecture is not simply an arrangement of functional parts and visual motifs, but also a meaningful record and symbol of the social values of a society and of aesthetic truth.

CHAPTER 9

AMERICA

Copley Square and the Concept of Architectural Ensemble

A building is a living exponent of a city. It is a thing complete in itself but also a component of a wider urban ensemble or collection of buildings in a constantly changing environment. As part of this complex urban tapestry, buildings in groupings such as Copley Square visually reflect and comment on each other, enriching the design of the city. A sense of ensemble, or of complementary inter-relationships of buildings, can lead toward a positive physical and psychological sense of place for the public. How can a city bring architectural order to urban chaos over a century of spatial, functional and stylistic change—a changing tapestry without monotony?

The complex task of balancing disparate forms is possible, as exhibited over two centuries by the buildings of Boston on Beacon Hill, in the Back Bay and in Copley Square. Similar scale of buildings, shapes, heights, colors of building materials, rhythmic repetition of similar façades and recurrent motifs can all contribute to creating a visual sense of urban order. Continuous and even building setbacks with sidewalks and trees create a calm, logical street scene. Mutual understanding among varied designs contributes to a sense of wholeness in an urban space. Respecting sunlight and shadow within the city also allows open spaces to become inviting places. Varied yet respectful architectural design, open space and landscape create the strong sense of urban ensemble we seek. As pedestrians, we perceive good urban ensemble when we experience it, consciously or unconsciously.

Copley Square

The Copley Square T station, part of the architectural ensemble, from Beaux-Arts to Modernism, that distinguishes Copley Square as a well-designed urban place.

As either Art Square (triangular) or Copley Square (rectangular), this place over a century has undergone multiple design and landscape iterations. From a tidal marsh (eighteenth century); to a crossroad of streets and streetcars, cut diagonally by a major avenue (nineteenth century); to an experimental, abstract sunken concrete composition below street level (1970s); to today's walkable green space with trees and benches, Copley Square has made every effort to become an integrated urban ensemble over time. Today, we are fortunate that this is now a place for contemporary people to interact, to live in the present, under historic landmark buildings. The aesthetic relationships of a city's architecture influence urban experience.

Architecture within urban space must speak with respect to other buildings to create aesthetic dialogue. Fortunately, visitors may notice that ensemble as an architectural issue has been addressed throughout the history of Copley Square. For example, the contemporary pink granite of Copley Place mall considerably turns its twentieth-century massive scale at an angle to nineteenth-century Copley Square—allowing it to be a participating but less obtrusive part of the ensemble of earlier buildings.

Like the pedestrian-friendly sidewalk shops along Boylston Street, commercial enterprises of stores, restaurants and hotels have become part of the American urban scene of Copley Square.

Three buildings of Copley Square, from the late nineteenth to the late twentieth century, in particular, should be noted for their success in creating this sense of ensemble for Copley Square, referring to the past yet being distinctive buildings of their own time. These ensemble buildings are: Old South Church, the Copley Plaza Hotel and the Johnson Building of the Boston Public Library.

Old South Church has an aesthetic affinity to Trinity Church diagonally across the square. Likewise, the Copley Plaza Hotel extends the Beaux-Arts style of the Boston Public Library. The Johnson Building is a contemporary design derivation of the McKim Building of the Boston Public Library. These relationships create a calm sense of ensemble and visual echo within Copley Square. The finest buildings in a city often have mutual relationships—architecture speaks to architecture.

Old South Church (circa 1875)
Cummings and Sears

A strangely beautiful, highly original Venetian Gothic Revival church lies somewhat hidden in a corner of Copley Square: Old South Church (Cummings and Sears, 1871–75). The Venetian campanile, or bell tower, rises with stunning verticality above Copley Square and particularly above its Beaux-Arts aesthetic opposition, the Boston Public Library. The relationship of these two very different buildings may at first sound visually contradictory, yet they are just far enough apart, across a busy street intersection, to complement each other, allowing us to enjoy the originality of the architecture of Old South Church.

Even more importantly for urban ensemble, Old South Church relates aesthetically to the Romanesque forms of Trinity Church, seen at a diagonal across Copley Square. Old South Church, like Trinity Church, moved to the newly created Copley Square in the 1870s. This compact, turreted church is unexpectedly ornate for a Congregational church; Italian Gothic would not be the expected motif for Protestantism. "It is designed in a style inspired by the architecture of medieval Venice," with "Venetian mosaics and stained glass windows of 15th century English Style."[57]

The colorful history of Old South Church has elements of a recanted Salem witch trial saga; strong abolitionist efforts; and the baptism of an American Patriot, Benjamin Franklin, statesman, library founder and European traveler. Even the building's previous name was historically memorable: "New Old South Church." With the congregation, Old South Church brought to Copley Square some significant historical roots, as well as one of the primary religious documents in America, *The Bay Psalm Book*, the "first book published in the Colonies."[58] The relationship of this book with its home in Copley Square reminds us that knowledge has always been celebrated in this Boston place.

One of the earliest American books and the first American public library share Copley Square. From the Venetian turrets of Old South Church, we cross the street to the Parisian Beaux-Arts design of the Boston Public Library. This church represents a true mélange of European influences on American forms of the late nineteenth century.[59] Old South Church seems to have derived its forms, in spite of its colonial Puritan values, from fashionable European aesthetic sources, particularly from British scholar John Ruskin's interpretations of the Venetian style. This building, a major contributor to the ensemble that we call Copley Square, can best be understood as reflecting "the free-wheeling individualism"[60] of an architectural era. Old South Church was listed in the National Register of Historic Places in 1970.

THE COPLEY PLAZA HOTEL (1912)
HENRY JANEWAY HARDENBURGH

It is a very difficult design challenge to stand between two major American landmarks: Copley Square's Trinity Church and the Boston Public Library. Yet the Fairmont Copley Plaza Hotel has accomplished this feat in a calmly controlled Beaux-Arts composition with a quietly dignified design. The interior is lavish and private, but the exterior respects and reflects the city square on which it sits. This hotel manages to link two major preexisting works of architecture in a relationship with its own gracefully drawn design, creating a sense of closure and urban ensemble exceptionally well.

The basic shape of this hotel is spreading and horizontal with a bow front, calmly symmetrical, yet decorative and demonstrative enough to invite guests inside. Note the repetitive windows and central entrance. These

Architectural ensemble in Copley Square.

design elements refer to, but do not copy, Trinity's and the library's lines of arched window forms and symmetrical entrances. The street entrance, the sweeping large-scale bow front, reflects the historic forms of the bow front town houses on Commonwealth Avenue in the Back Bay. While the use of decorative ornament and white stone persists from the past, it is found here in simplified classical shape.

Stylistically, the Copley Plaza was designed in an interesting time: the Early Modern era, from the turn of the twentieth century to the 1920s. Older established Beaux-Arts architectural motifs were still respected and well executed, yet the simplicity of Modernism was just entering architecture. The European Beaux-Arts and Early Modern American styles together influence the Copley Plaza Hotel. It is both clean and classical in tone, displaying a correctly approachable but sophisticated façade to Copley Square. This hotel design is a proper private foil for its architecturally noted neighboring landmark edifices. It is also well sited for a hotel, forming one side of an important pedestrian square, within walking distance of public transit and the Amtrak trains of Back Bay station. This is how private urban ensemble architecture can quietly complement the city environment. The National Trust for Historic Preservation named the Fairmont Copley Plaza one of the Historic Hotels of America in 1989.

The Johnson Building of the Boston Public Library (1972)
Philip Johnson

The three giant granite arches of the Johnson Building of the Boston Public Library, adjoining Copley Square along Boylston Street, extend the nineteenth century into the twentieth century as architecture, commenting on the continuity of Classicism in architecture. Here, architect Philip Johnson faced an aesthetically difficult challenge for any architect: to build an annex to one of the most important buildings in America, Charles McKim's original Beaux-Arts Boston Public Library. Johnson's solution was simple and insightful, particularly in that it comprehends the significance of its predecessor and tries to conform aesthetically.

The Johnson Building mirrors the size, scale, materials, roofline and street setback of the McKim Building. It also makes a very strong reference to McKim's use of arches on the façade—a visual and historical form prevalent throughout Copley Square. Johnson observed the adjoining McKim model and responded with his own building, based on McKim's work, with a giant rectangular box pierced with oversized arches. Johnson, of course, was working within an era that did not allow for the handmade detail of McKim's day, and thus Johnson chose to define his modern building with unadorned, simplified modern geometric forms.

It appears to this author that Johnson was also creating an original critical commentary on Beaux-Arts Neo-Classicism. Noting that McKim and the Beaux-Arts were in their time a recall of the architecture of Classical antiquity, it certainly seems that Johnson understood that he was working both in the antique and the modern for this commission. As a curator of architecture, Johnson well knew that the Beaux-Arts style was based on historical precedent. Johnson's new style of twentieth-century Modernism also recalls the nineteenth-century recall of Beaux-Arts Classicism, becoming a kind of unusual "Neo-Neo-Classicism," commenting on McKim's original Neo-Classical library. This building illustrates Philip Johnson's design development and personal commentary on architecture, moving the

The Johnson Building of the Boston Public Library. Its massive arches now overlook the trees of Boylston Street, just outside Copley Square.

architectural profession with him stylistically in the late twentieth century from Modernism into Post-Modernism.

With historian Henry-Russell Hitchcock, Johnson had earlier defined Modernism in *The International Style* as the prevalent white box or glass and steel skeletal architecture of the early decades of the twentieth century; their definitions strongly influenced architecture from 1932 into the 1960s postwar era. The tenets of the International Style delineated by Hitchcock and Johnson were: modern architecture emphasizes volume rather than mass; modern architecture is based on asymmetrical balance rather than on symmetry; modern architecture shows an absence of applied ornament; and modern architecture displays the articulation of structure.

With his own buildings, however, Johnson felt free, in time, to leave these rigid rules behind, becoming one of the first architects to defy such rules as he himself had invented. This author believes that sometimes Johnson was daring the art critics, with humor and irony, with his own contradictory styles. Rather than stay in the pure Modernist mode, he became historicizing, that is to say, he began to make his designs echo aspects of the history of architecture—history that he himself had considered inappropriate for the modern era in his earlier curatorial work. Here in Copley Square, Johnson was resolving many of the complex architectural contradictions with which he grappled in his theories, creating a building that is at once modern and historical in its allusions.

Architect of the Johnson Building, Philip Johnson

Philip Johnson (1906–2005) was a major modern American theorist, architect and winner of the prestigious gold medal of the American Institute of Architects in 1978 and the Pritzker Prize in architecture in 1979.[61] His Early Modernist credentials and mentors were highly reputable: he had worked with renowned German Modernist Mies van der Rohe on the Seagram Building in New York City, and he studied at Harvard's School of Design during the tenure of German émigré Modernist and Bauhaus founder Walter Gropius.

Even more interesting, however, was Johnson's early career as architecture curator of the Museum of Modern Art, New York City, where he coauthored *The International Style* (1932), the exhibition and book that defined early to mid-century European Modernism, with architectural historian Henry-Russell Hitchcock. Though Johnson wrote here of the simplicity of form of this style, he went on to look to more decorative architectural models for his own later work. From his early International-Style Modernism with Mies to the historicizing work of his later Post-Modernism, Johnson always sought to bring style, and sometimes wit and irony, to contemporary American architecture.

In addition to the Boston Public Library, in New England one can see a number of this architect's Modern and Post-Modern works. A side view of a late decorative Johnson building, known as 500 Boylston Street, designed with architect John Burgee (1989), is now visible behind the tower of Trinity Church above Copley Square. Much earlier, in his Modernist period, Philip Johnson designed a small private house for himself near Brattle Street in Cambridge, Massachusetts; his larger Modernist private residence compound, known as the Glass House, in New Canaan, Connecticut (1949), is open to the public with reservations.

Philip Johnson had previously created designs for Lincoln Center for the Performing Arts in New York City (mid-1960s), another ensemble of modern urban buildings designed in a quasi-Classical style.[62] Interestingly, Lincoln

Center uses a Renaissance configuration for its plan and arrangement of performance spaces. The mid-career styles of Philip Johnson, including, in particular, the Johnson Building of the Boston Public Library, extend Johnson's lifelong oeuvre, widening his architectural development from Mid-Century Modernism to a new kind of retro-Classicism that eventually came to be known as Post-Modernism. He is fortunate to be a namesake of the Johnson Building, a rare honor for an architect that the Boston Public Library has extended to him.

Another Kind of Architectural Ensemble: The Boston Public Library as Inspiration for Other Libraries in America

The American democratic meaning and the French Beaux-Arts style of the Boston Public Library were inspirational to many important libraries in major cities across the United States. The concepts and aesthetics of the Boston Public Library made this institution a leader among American libraries of the late nineteenth and early twentieth centuries. The Boston Public Library was the prime mover of the Beaux-Arts style for libraries and museums, transporting the style directly from Paris to Boston and then from Boston all over urban America. You may also wish to visit the following landmark Beaux-Arts American libraries. When you see these buildings, recall that they all share a common lineage with the Boston Public Library—a special relationship. These libraries together create a larger kind of ensemble of American Beaux-Arts architecture:

The Morgan Library, New York

The most significant visual comparison that one might make with the Boston Public Library is in New York City: the Morgan Library, by McKim, Mead & White (1906). The Morgan Library shares the sophisticated and controlled opulence of architect Charles Follen McKim's designs with his work in Boston.

The New York Public Library

A major building for which the Boston Public Library set a design standard is the New York Public Library, by the famous Beaux-Arts firm of Carrere & Hastings (1922). Also significant in New York City is the Frick Art Reference

Library by John Russell Pope (1935), who later became the Classical architect of the National Gallery in Washington, D.C. (1941).

The San Francisco Public Library
Proof of the wide influence of the Boston Public Library and its Beaux-Arts style in America is seen at the original San Francisco Public Library building (1916), now the Asian Art Museum of San Francisco. How interesting that European Beaux-Arts design principles spread from Paris to Boston, Chicago and New York and on to San Francisco, where European style now houses Asian arts in America. Thus, a style has traveled the continents.

Arches and Inspiration Renewed

The Boston Public Library has recently improved upon Johnson's Post-Modernist work while advancing its mission to the contemporary reading public. The interior renovation (2016) and rethinking of the more informal spaces of the Johnson Building, by the firm William Rawn Associates, has greatly improved, updated and enlivened the atmosphere for the library reader, as well as for the Boston pedestrian.

The new entry and open space of the Johnson Building of the Boston Public Library, overlooking the finish line for the traditional Boston Marathon, is now an approachable public space. At last, it has been redesigned for natural light and a closer relationship to the public street, with a line of trees, connected visually to Copley Square, exploring the previously unexploited potential of architect Philip Johnson's giant Post-Modern arched building on Boylston Street, adjoining Copley Square.

It is particularly interesting to think about the Johnson Building's visual emphasis on those giant arches. Arches have run thematically throughout Copley Square, from Richardson's Trinity Church arches, to McKim's arches in the front portals and in the Courtyard of the Boston Public Library, to Johnson's giant library arches. Eventually, abstract Modernist wooden arches appeared even in the design by architects Kallmann McKinnell and Wood for Boston's Back Bay station (1987), just beyond Copley, symbolizing that train stations are again beginning to command the respect this architectural form deserves as portal to the city.

The arch as architectural form—both as structural and as aesthetic element—has stood symbolically for millennia in Europe, and now here in America, for over a century, as it echoes around Boston's Copley Square. Search Copley Square for its repeated arches. The repetition of these forms helps to create, consciously and unconsciously, the sense of a unified urban composition through architectural ensemble that we seek in a public square.

CHAPTER 10

AMERICA

The Skyscraper and the Square

THE HANCOCK TOWER, I.M. PEI AND ASSOCIATES (CIRCA 1975)

If Trinity Church is thought of as a metaphorical stone mountain over Copley Square, then the Hancock Tower can be conceived of as the sky and the cumulus clouds suspended high above that mountain, reflecting in its glass the whole environment of the city and the sky. A giant prism, it reflects and refracts clouds, sky and city lights. The Hancock Tower defines for Boston the concept of the International Style skyscraper: a tall, gridded glass and steel structure, significant in its sleek shape, a landmark in its urban site—abstract, urban and urbane.

    An icon of Mid-Century American Modernism—that was itself based on early European Modernism—the Hancock Tower stands in view of both the European-influenced Romanesque Trinity Church and the French Beaux-Arts Boston Public Library. Fortunately for this historic city, this is an excellent example of the complexities of architectural context, in which contrasting European and American styles are sited next to each other, gracefully resolved. Style, mass, materials, height and meaning fortunately were handled here by a subtle and insightful architect, I.M. Pei, with "classic restraint," in the words of Hitchcock and Johnson's *The International Style*.[63]

The Hancock Tower, by architect I.M. Pei, reflecting Trinity Church and the sky and clouds above Boston. *Photo by K.F.K. Cormier.*

History through Architecture

Architect of the Hancock Tower, I.M. Pei

I.M. Pei (b. 1917) is a premier modern architect of twentieth-century America and the International Style, winner of the gold medal of AIA in 1979 and the Pritzker Prize in 1983.[64] He exemplifies the concept of America as a place of talented émigrés, having been born in China. He, too, studied at Harvard's School of Design during the tenure of Walter Gropius, an earlier artistic émigré. We are fortunate that this talented international architect was wisely selected by the corporation to create a major landmark visible over Copley Square and from most of the cities of Boston, Cambridge and environs. How different and less refined Copley Square would be today if left in the hands of lesser modern architects than I.M. Pei and his design partners.

The Hancock speaks to American corporate material aspirations, a representation of the booming postwar American economy. It is fortunate that this corporation, named after an American Patriot and early businessman, chose to leave its mark on this city via a positive symbol of its American success. Certainly not all our corporate architecture, within Boston and many other American cities, has been so considerate or well designed. The glass and steel grid and, in particular, the blue-green glass reflectivity of the Hancock Tower define the Modern era not only in Copley Square but in Boston as a whole. As this book is being written, we congratulate architect I.M. Pei, who is celebrating his 100th birthday…yet still so modern!

Compare the subtle placement and shape of this Pei building to other, less creative urban skyscrapers you see in this and other cities to appreciate Pei's graceful design of "truly classic restraint." These qualities were explained by the partner of I.M. Pei, architect Henry Cobb. Note that Cobb emphasizes how deferential the design of their firm's Modernist approach is to the historical building of Trinity Church, as they stand next to each other, at an angle, in Copley Square: "The tower's uniformly gridded and reflective surface…mutes the obtrusiveness…and defers in all respects to the rich sculptural qualities of its much smaller neighbor." The architects were "shaping the tower in such a way that the church becomes the autonomous center and the tower the contingent satellite in the composition."[65] Such stylistic restraint and admirable aesthetic modesty of the architect show real respect for the meaning and composition of Copley Square and thus were significant; however, the building of sixty stories once created quite a controversy. Copley Square is, for America, antique in site and scale.

By its nature, a skyscraper is a thing of the modern world, its construction not even possible before the twentieth century. Thus, there was a need for the modern designer to invent an aesthetic to express this edifice to the world in which it is constructed, as towers literally began to tower over cities, defining a wholly new aesthetic for Boston and other major cities. The Modernism of Copley Square, fortunately, is the work of a master of American architecture. Its 1970s design stylistically traced its theories and forms to the Early Modernism of Europe and its creativity. The most innovative architecture of the twentieth century was often found in advances in skyscraper design.

In the opinion of this author, Pei's vision for Boston's skyscraper in Copley Square hearkens back to the visual and theoretical influence of the Early Modernism of architect Mies van der Rohe, as seen today in the Museum of Modern Art in New York. Mies's stunning early charcoal renderings of designs for a glass skyscraper, drawn fifty years before the Hancock Tower, certainly would have been visual precedents for Pei.[66] Totally Modern and American in his approach to glass and steel, I.M. Pei was not afraid to reflect, literally, the historical architecture of Trinity Church, nor to reflect upon, as precedent, Early Modern European architecture for his new American skyscraper.

Reflection, Color and Shape in Copley Square

Clearly, this skyscraper design represents a very different viewpoint from Copley's previous civic architecture for public institutions. Here in Copley Square, Pei has demonstrated the concept of visual oppositions—mass versus volume, horizontality versus verticality. The glass of the Hancock Tower represents the aesthetic opposite of the stones of Trinity. The tall geometric form of the Hancock is likewise the opposite of the low cubic Boston Public Library.

Employing aesthetic oppositions shows that it is possible to respect the historical forms of Copley without copying them. The finest modern architecture respects, but does not imitate, earlier architecture. This skyscraper is inventive yet simple, true to its own era.

Truth of form is an important concept of the Modern. A glass tower, for any city, is a very modern thing—an unprecedented form—particularly for a city like Boston with its historical architecture and scale. How fortunate that this breakthrough skyscraper is also a work of art—a prismatic, geometric, turquoise-blue glass object that is artistically complete in itself and still more significant within its complicated urban context. It is simple, in the best sense of the word. Its design is not boring, nor is it egotistical or willful. This skyscraper in Copley Square is a structurally and aesthetically unified and masterful gesture. Compare the subtle placement and overall shape of this Pei building to other, less creative urban skyscrapers you see in cities to fully appreciate Pei's graceful design of "truly classic restraint."

The subtlety of Pei's design lies in its reflectivity, its shape, its color and its aesthetic contradictions. This Copley Square building is, like glass, both solid material but also, due to atmospheric conditions, often transparent or almost invisible. Metaphorically, it becomes the clouds over Boston it reflects. In the famous words of Pei's predecessor, the architect Mies van der Rohe, "Architecture is almost nothing."

Clouds and Symbols

The best view of Boston's Hancock Tower is not actually from Copley Square, though this is surely beautiful in situ. To take in this glass prism visually, cross the Charles River to Cambridge to view the skyline from the pedestrian walkway along Memorial Drive. There, from the grassy walk along the river, the tower is seen in its full power—its geometry, its placement in the skyline, its unique color and, most impressively, its reflectivity. You may be there just at the moment that the reflection of white clouds and blue sky creates an optical illusion: the building appears to vanish, to disappear and reappear. It seems to become only the sky it reflects.

Its color is turquoise-blue, but it also visually reflects the earth colors of the stones of Trinity Church, as seen on the cover of this book. The author also notes that the striking, unique color of the glass of the Hancock Tower is a distinctive creative choice that may also historically reflect the church building. As this unusual turquoise-blue glass relates the building to the New England sky, it also subtly recalls, perhaps unconsciously, the rare turquoise-colored glass of its neighbor Trinity Church, with its massive opalescent stained glass of La Farge's *Christ in Majesty* window.

Only the finest glass skyscrapers of Modernism aspire to be aesthetic objects that enhance an urban environment. Pei's Modern architecture has become for Boston an object of modern urban art. Its exterior shape as a reflective blue crystalline object above the surrounding city is viewed as sculpture is viewed in a museum—an object set within space to be appreciated as a pure abstract geometric form.

In the words of architectural historian William H. Jordy, "The 'glass' skyscraper was, indeed, the consummate vision of the International Style.... In these towers, glass predominated in a double sense: literally and symbolically."[67]

Creating Contemporary Architecture to Complement Historic Copley Square

Like the estuary Boston had once been, the artistic tides of architecture were at last, by the mid-twentieth century, reversing, now flowing back, in the opposite direction, as Modernism moved from America to Europe.

As we have seen in the previous chapters, Boston, for more than a century, had been strongly influenced by European architectural styles and urban design. Particularly significant for its importation of style in Copley Square had been the Boston Public Library, American example of the French Beaux-Arts, a style that itself had looked back toward earlier Italian Renaissance sources.

America at last assumed the global architectural lead via advances in Mid-Century Modern skyscraper design. World focus by necessity had moved from Europe toward the dynamism of the American building boom, from the mid-twentieth century into the early twenty-first century. I.M. Pei and the Hancock Tower were thus important touch points in this American Modern movement, a style with its roots in Early European Modernism.

Often the most difficult problems in urban design, magnified in the modern era, concern the concepts of truth—of architectural form, of era and of urban context. This search means endeavoring to create a building true to its own time yet also respectful of its preexisting historical urban context. Pei's modern American skyscraper towers today in Copley Square above the historical European-influenced architecture of Richardson's Romanesque and McKim's Beaux-Arts, yet it stands calmly and with insight. "The great modern architects have known how to achieve interest in their compositions while exercising a truly classic restraint."[68]

Over a century of design, Copley Square has made strides in answering the basic questions of integrating styles, both European and American, into the square. Sensitive contemporary architecture—truthful to its time yet within historical context—creates the city as an organic, living place.

CONCLUSION

AMERICA AND EUROPE

Finding Form in the Square

Celebrating the Square in the City

There are major points we can learn from Copley Square and its one-hundred-year history of architecture and urban design. Among these are aspiring always to excellence in architecture; respecting human visual viewpoint in design; understanding the sense of architectural openness and enclosure in cities; cultivating the relationship of urban space to nature; and continuing to welcome international advances in urban style into America. It is key to urban design success to acknowledge that a city is a living human place—not simply a place to pass through to another place or an abstraction of objects in space.

Architecture: Americans should always demand excellence in the architecture of our cities, for it is well within our reach, as we have seen in Boston's Copley Square. Charles Follen McKim's Boston Public Library is historical proof that our civic buildings can be artistic reflections of our finest American ideas and ideals, as well as creative summations of styles learned outside America. Contemporary architecture, as exemplified by I.M. Pei's visually sophisticated International Style, too, can aspire to create excellence in Modern American design. Our cities will live up to these aesthetic standards only if we, as a people, set and maintain our civic architectural standards high.

Conclusion

Boston's Copley Square and the Hancock Tower, viewed from Cambridge, Massachusetts, across the Charles River. *Photo by K.F.K. Cormier.*

Visual Viewpoint and Sound: Humans view the world and partake of their environment through their senses. We encounter the city at our own eye and ear level. Though we may feel energized by a background din of a city, invasive noise must be controlled in the pedestrian urban environment. Architecture and urban design must take the eye-level pedestrian viewpoint as the starting point (at four to six feet above the ground), rather than viewing urban spaces from above or from a moving vehicle. Boston has learned this lesson through years of urban design corrections and iterations.

Enclosure and Open Space: Humans want to relax and enjoy open space with urban amenity, such as benches, in cities, but urban open spaces must specifically accommodate themselves to the human sense of safe enclosure. We instinctively want to see around us while also feeling that we are covered. This is why the courtyard with fountain, or the street-front café on the busy boulevard, or the pedestrian square as urban form have persisted and enticed civilizations from antique to contemporary times, from Rome to Paris to London to Boston.

Conclusion

Nature and Trees: This author is convinced that though we may not always be conscious of this deep primeval human need—our relationship to nature and to trees, and to sunlight and shade, to fresh air, to the shapes and colors of nature—we are better people when we live with trees around us. Not only because the urban landscape creates comfort, as it does, but we must also appreciate the fact that trees influence microclimates. They cool and freshen our steel and concrete cities naturally, and they complement even our human breath as trees inhale carbon dioxide and exhale oxygen into our lungs and our urban environments. Only through nature can we create the urban oasis we seek.

Therefore, to enhance the contemporary American city, give us pedestrian squares of trees, benches, sky, enclosure and openness, with eye-level interest. Add a café and a safe place for children to play. Humane places in old European cities point the way that Copley Square, in Boston's Back Bay, has learned—from London's Bloomsbury squares to Paris's cafes on the Champs-Élysées.

A humane environment and an urban oasis, Copley Square today.

Conclusion

Copley Square as Café American

Now…imagine cappuccino in the shadow of the Pantheon in Rome, or Perrier on the Rue du Bac in Paris, or afternoon tea in Russell Square in London, or just a paper cup of American coffee under the shade trees in Copley Square. This is the calm and joyful pedestrian life that Copley Square can emulate from Europe's long pedestrian urban design history. The most engaging European café life, enjoyed in streets and tree-shaded squares, is the experience owed to all people, including Americans, in our cities. This is what a city can be in America—this is Café American.

We must seek to maintain or to create the spirit of the city, and that is found in the careful balance of chaos within order, of humans within the urban environment. Classical models of public open space have been thriving in Rome and Paris and London for centuries. We can continue to learn to make our American cities into humane pedestrian spaces. We can transfer the finest ancient European and innovative American urban configurations to our cities, embrace human scale and design enlightened spaces within our contemporary American cities and squares.

Cities are complex and chaotic yet also, at best, personal and peaceful. These places are the confluence of geometry with nature. They carry

Confetti flies over Copley Square as Boston celebrates! *Photo by K.F.K. Cormier.*

Conclusion

in their architecture messages from our historical past, we inhabit their contemporary constructions, walking their cobblestones and pavement today, in the knowledge that these urban agglomerations will formulate our global future.

Here in Boston's Copley Square is a century of European architecture in America. Without crossing an ocean, we can simply come to this place in the city, to Copley Square, to this urban oasis. This urbane place endures as the most European, and yet also perhaps the most American, place in America.

A GLOSSARY OF ART AND ARCHITECTURAL TERMS

ANTECEDENT: a significant work that has gone before; an architectural precedent

ANTIQUITY: the era and style of ancient Greece and Rome

APSE: the east end of a church, where the altar is situated behind the choir

ARCH: a curved architectural element between two columns, held in balance by a keystone; arches can be Roman, Gothic or Romanesque in style

ARCUATED: composed of arches

BEAUX-ARTS STYLE: nineteenth-century French architectural style based on forms of Classical architecture (pronounced "Boz-Ar")

CLASSICAL ARCHITECTURE: the era and style of ancient Greece and Rome

COLONNADE: a passageway created by a row of columns

COLOSSEUM: Roman architectural site, used as precedent for later European architects

A Glossary of Art and Architectural Terms

École des Beaux-Arts: School of the Fine Arts, Paris, for the rigorous training of architects; literally, School of the Beautiful Arts (pronounced "A-Cole-Day-Boz-Ar")

Façade: elevation or exterior wall of a building (pronounced "Fa-sod")

Gothic arch: a pointed arch based on medieval Gothic or Gothic Revival churches

The Grand Tour: extended travel throughout Europe, from England or France to the Classical sites of Italy or Greece, for the educated and privileged of the seventeenth through the nineteenth centuries

International Style: the major style of twentieth-century Modern architecture, most often seen in urban skyscrapers

Modern style: the major architectural style of the twentieth century in Europe and America, based on simplicity of form, as logical expression of function

Mural: an elongated, narrative painting, attached to a wall, usually found on public architecture

Narthex: the entrance hall to a church or cathedral

The Orders: Classical architectural forms, including Doric, Ionic and Corinthian Orders

Piazza: plaza

Post and lintel: a simple form of building, with two vertical post supports, holding one horizontal lintel across the upright posts

Post-Modern: architecture after Modernism, often commenting on the Modern in an ironic way

A Glossary of Art and Architectural Terms

PRECEDENT: antecedent or architectural form that preexists a structure, for which it is used as a model; the Classical architecture of Greece and Rome became the precedent for the Italian Renaissance, as well as for eighteenth- and nineteenth-century American architecture

RENAISSANCE: literally, the "rebirth" of Classical form; in architecture, this often refers to works of the fifteenth and sixteenth centuries in Rome and Florence

ROMANESQUE: Roman-like architecture, using rounded arches; this style preceded the use of pointed arches

NOTES

Introduction

1. U.S. National Park Service, nps.gov/nr.
2. Tyler, Ligibel and Tyler, *Historic Preservation*, 160–64.

Chapter 1

3. Whitehall and Kennedy, *Boston*, 5.
4. Chamberlain, *Beacon Hill*, 31.
5. Trinity Church in the City of Boston, self-guided tour.
6. Chamberlain, *Beacon Hill*.
7. Ibid., 50.
8. Whitehall and Kennedy, *Boston*, 111.
9. Baigell, *Concise History of American Painting*, 24.
10. See examples of Copley's works in America at the Boston Museum of Fine Arts and the Metropolitan Museum of Art, New York, and in England at the Courtauld Institute, Somerset House, London.
11. The sculptor is Lewis Cohen, for the Friends of Copley Square.
12. Old South Church, see brochure and www.oldsouth.org.
13. Tyler, Ligibel and Tyler, *Historic Preservation*.

Chapter 2

14. Drexler, *Architecture of the École des Beaux-Arts*, preface, 8.
15. Sullivan, "Tall Office Building Artistically Considered."

Chapter 3

16. Friends of Copley Square website.
17. Ibid.
18. As readers may be aware, unfortunately, Marathon Monday was disrupted by violence on April 15, 2013, at the finish line on Boylston Street outside the Johnson Building of the Boston Public Library. In this horrific attack, 3 people, including a child, were killed and over 250 injured. See articles in the *Boston Globe* newspaper for details. The city has recovered, and the Marathon continues.
19. Berenson, *Boston and the Civil War*, 69.
20. Hitchcock, *Architecture of H.H. Richardson*, 145.
21. Wick, *Art and Architecture of the Boston Public Library*, 5.
22. Berenson, *Boston and the Civil War*, 69.

Chapter 4

23. Ruskin, "Influence of Imagination," 176.
24. Trinity Church brochure.
25. O'Gorman, *Makers of Trinity Church*, Morgan, introduction, 3.
26. Tyler, Ligibel and Tyler, *Historic Preservation*, 78.
27. Ruskin, "Influence of Imagination," 180.
28. Ruskin, *St. Mark's Rest*, 94.
29. Ruskin, *The Unity of Art*, 79.

Chapter 5

30. Hitchcock, *Architecture of H.H. Richardson*, 145–46.
31. Ibid.
32. Ibid.
33. Drexler, *Architecture of the École des Beaux-Arts*, 466.

34. Van Zanten, "Architectural Composition at the École des Beaux-Arts," 185.
35. *New York Times*, September 23, 1894.
36. A curatorial comparison of the stained glass of La Farge and Tiffany, by style and technique, can be seen in the American Wing of the Museum of Fine Arts, Boston.
37. Ruskin, *Unity of Art*, 58.

Chapter 6

38. Cormier, "Urban Planning," 1379–82.
39. Hogarth, *Walking Tours of Old Boston*, 71.
40. Chamberlain, *Beacon Hill*, 200–1.
41. See www.boston.gov/historic-district/back-bay-architectural-district.
42. Ruskin, *Stones of Venice*.

Chapter 7

43. Wick, *Art and Architecture of the Boston Public Library*, 12–13.
44. Ibid.
45. The Boston Public Library, sculptor Bela Lyon Pratt (1867–1917).
46. Selected Library Special Collections, approximately chronological, some longer titles edited.
47. Roth, *McKim, Mead & White*, 6.
48. Ibid.

Chapter 8

49. *New York Times*, September 23, 1894.
50. Roth, *McKim, Mead & White*, 115.
51. Jordy, *American Buildings and Their Architects: Progressive and Academic Ideals*, 337–43.
52. Ibid.
53. Boston Public Library, brochure.
54. Jordy, *American Buildings and Their Architects: Progressive and Academic Ideals*, 364.

55. Drexler, *Architecture of the École des Beaux-Arts*, 61.
56. *New York Times*, September 23, 1894.

Chapter 9

57. Old South Church, brochure.
58. Ibid.
59. Boston Architectural College, architectural drawings collection.
60. Jordy, *American Buildings and Their Architects: Progressive and Academic Ideals*.
61. Pritzker Prize, www.pritzkerprize.com.
62. Cormier, "Lincoln Center."

Chapter 10

63. Hitchcock and Johnson, *International Style*, 59.
64. Pritzer Prize.
65. Comments by Henry Cobb, Harvard GSD lecture, 1980. Pei Cobb Freed & Partners website. Henry N. Cobb and Harold Fredenburgh, lead designers, Hancock Tower (planning 1967, construction 1968, completion 1976) (building now known as 200 Clarendon Street).
66. These dramatic 1922 charcoal drawings for a glass skyscraper can be viewed at the Museum of Modern Art in New York City.
67. Jordy, "The Laconic Splendor of the Metal Frame: Mies van der Rohe," *American Buildings and Their Architects*, vol. 4, 232.
68. Hitchcock and Johnson, *International Style*.

BIBLIOGRAPHY

American Academy in Rome. McKim, Mead & White. www.aarome.org.

American National Biography. 24 vols. New York: Oxford University Press, 1999.

Baigell, Matthew. *A Concise History of American Painting and Sculpture*. New York: Harper & Row, Publishers, 1984.

Berenson, Barbara F. *Boston and the Civil War: Hub of the Second Revolution*. Charleston, SC: The History Press, 2014.

Boston Architectural Library, architectural archives, drawings of Old South Church by architects Cummings and Sears.

Boston Public Library. www.bpl.org.

Brooks, Phillips (1835–1893). "Papers of Phillips Brooks: An Inventory." Harvard University Library, 2016. oasis.lib.harvard.edu.

Chafee, Richard. "The Teaching of Architecture at the École Des Beaux-Arts." In *The Architecture of the École des Beaux-Arts*. Exhibition catalogue with essays, Museum of Modern Art, NYC. Cambridge, MA: MIT Press, 1977, 61.

Chamberlain, Allen. *Beacon Hill: Its Ancient Pastures and Early Mansions*. Boston: Riverside Press, 1925.

Cormier, Leslie Humm. "Urban Planning" and "Lincoln Center," in *Encyclopedia of 20th Century Architecture*, edited by R. Stephen Sennott. New York: Fitzroy Dearborn, Taylor & Francis Books, 2004.

Curtis, William J.R.R. *Modern Architecture Since 1900*. Oxford, UK: Phaidon Press, 1987.

Bibliography

Drexler, Arthur, ed. *The Architecture of the École des Beaux-Arts*. Exhibition catalogue with essays, Museum of Modern Art, NYC. Cambridge, MA: MIT Press, 1977.

———. "Beaux-Arts Buildings in France and America." In *The Architecture of the École des Beaux-Arts*. Exhibition catalogue with essays, Museum of Modern Art, NYC. Cambridge, MA: MIT Press, 1977, 417.

———. "Engineer's Architecture: Truth and Its Consequences." In *The Architecture of the École des Beaux-Arts*. Exhibition catalogue with essays, Museum of Modern Art, NYC. Cambridge, MA: MIT Press, 1977, 13.

Friends of Copley Square. friendsofcopleysquare.org.

Heine, Florian, and Isabel Kuhl. *The Buildings that Revolutionized Architecture*. New York and London: Prestel, 2015.

Hitchcock, Henry-Russell. *The Architecture of H.H. Richardson and His Times*. Cambridge, MA: MIT Press, 1981.

Hitchcock, Henry-Russell, and Philip Johnson. *The International Style*. With an essay by Alfred Barr. New York: Museum of Modern Art, 1932.

Hogarth, Paul. *Walking Tours of Old Boston*. N.p.: Dutton Books, 1978.

Jordy, William H. *American Buildings and Their Architects: Progressive and Academic Ideals at the Turn of the Twentieth Century*. Vol. 3. Garden City, NY: Anchor Press/Doubleday, 1976.

———. *American Buildings and Their Architects: The Impact of European Modernism in the Mid-Twentieth Century*. Vol. 4. Garden City, NY: Anchor Press/Doubleday, 1976.

Levine, Neil. "The Romantic Idea of Architectural Legibility: Henri Labrouste and the Neo-Grec." In *The Architecture of the École des Beaux-Arts*. Exhibition catalogue with essays, Museum of Modern Art, NYC. Cambridge, MA: MIT Press, 1977, 325.

Metropolitan Museum of Art, Heilbrunn Timeline of Art History, New York. www.metmuseum.org.

Muthesius, Stefan. *The English Terraced House*. London: Yale University Press, 1982.

National Park Service. "National Historic Landmarks Program." www.nps.gov/nhl.

National Trust for Historic Preservation. "Historic Hotels of America." www.historichotels.

New York Times. "Boston's New Public Library, One of the Handsomest Buildings in the Unites States, It Occupies a Commanding Site in Copley Square." September 23, 1894.

Bibliography

O'Gorman, James F., ed., introduction by Keith N. Morgan. *The Makers of Trinity Church in the City of Boston*. Amherst: University of Massachusetts Press, 2004.

Old South Church in Boston. "History." www.oldsouth.org/about/history.

Pei, I.M. "Pei Cobb Freed & Partners." www.pcf-p.com/projects/john-hancock-tower.

Roth, Leland M. *McKim, Mead & White, Architects*. New York: Harper & Row Publishers, 1983.

Ruskin, John. "The Influence of Imagination." Lecture to the Architectural Association, London, 1857, Senate House Library, University of London.

———. *The Seven Lamps of Architecture*, 1849; *The Stones of Venice*, 1851; *The Unity of Art*, 1859; *St. Mark's Rest*, 1877. Ruskin books and publications, Special Collections, Senate House Library, University of London, UK.

Sullivan, Louis. "The Tall Office Building Artistically Considered." Essay, 1896.

Trinity Church in the City of Boston. Self-guided tour, illustrated brochure and website. www.trinitychurchboston.org.

Tyler, Norman, Ted J. Ligibel and Ilene R. Tyler. *Historic Preservation: An Introduction to Its History, Principles, and Practice*. 2nd ed. New York: W.W. Norton & Company, 2009.

Van Zanten, David. "Architectural Composition at the École des Beaux-Arts from Charles Percier to Charles Garnier." In *The Architecture of the École des Beaux-Arts*. Exhibition catalogue with essays, Museum of Modern Art, NYC. Cambridge, MA: MIT Press, 1977, 111.

Wells Cathedral, Somerset, UK. www.wellscathedral.org.uk.

Whitehall, Walter Muir, and Lawrence W. Kennedy. *Boston: A Topographical History*. Cambridge, MA: Belknap Press of Harvard University Press, 2000.

Wick, Peter Arms. *A Handbook to the Art and Architecture of the Boston Public Library: Visitors Guide to the McKim Building, Copley Square, Its Mural Decorations and Its Collections*. Photographs by Richard Cheek. Boston: Associates of the Boston Public Library, 1977.

INDEX

A

arches 31, 36, 51, 55, 56, 60, 66, 92, 93, 98, 106, 110, 111, 125, 127

B

Back Bay 15, 19, 20, 23, 24, 25, 32, 36, 41, 42, 43, 44, 46, 49, 52, 69, 71, 74, 76, 78, 80, 90, 101, 105, 110, 121
Beacon Hill 17, 19, 20, 24, 25, 26, 29, 30, 32, 72, 74, 76, 87, 101
Beaux-Arts, L'École des 37, 84, 96, 98
Beaux-Arts, style 15, 17, 21, 31, 36, 37, 38, 45, 52, 63, 71, 75, 76, 77, 78, 83, 85, 89, 94, 96, 97, 98, 99, 103, 104, 105, 106, 109, 110, 113, 118, 125, 126
Bloomsbury squares 18, 72, 121
Boston Common 19, 44, 71, 78, 81
Boston Public Library 12, 17, 18, 20, 36, 37, 38, 39, 41, 45, 46, 47, 52, 54, 71, 78, 81, 82, 83, 84, 85, 86, 87, 89, 90, 91, 93, 94, 95, 96, 98, 99, 100, 103, 104, 106, 108, 109, 110, 113, 118, 119
Brooks, Phillips 47, 49, 50, 52, 54
Brunelleschi, Filippo 98, 99
Bulfinch, Charles 26, 27, 33, 34, 35

C

canals 66
Cancelleria 98, 99
Central Park (NYC) 76, 79, 80
Classical architecture 39, 125, 127
Commonwealth Avenue 18, 25, 52, 71, 76, 105
Copley, John Singleton 26, 28, 29, 30, 33, 34, 35

Index

Copley Plaza Hotel 20, 31, 39, 71, 103, 104, 105
Courtyard of the Boston Public Library 96, 98, 100, 110
Cummings and Sears 20, 37, 67, 103

F

500 Boylston Street. *See* Johnson Building, the
Florence, Italy 18, 34, 89, 93, 97, 98, 127

G

Gilman, Arthur 71, 76
Grand Tour 15, 33, 34, 35, 40, 126

H

Hancock Tower 17, 18, 38, 39, 71, 113, 115, 116, 117, 118
Haussmann, Georges-Eugène, Baron 70, 76
Haussmann Plan. *See* Haussmann, Georges-Eugène, Baron
historic preservation 21, 27, 31
Hitchcock and Johnson 107, 113
Hitchcock, Henry-Russell 59, 107, 108, 113

I

International Style 16, 107, 108, 113, 115, 118, 119, 126

J

Johnson Building, the 45, 83, 103, 106, 108, 109, 110
Johnson, Philip 106, 107, 108, 110
Jordy, William H. 90, 95, 118

L

La Farge, John 54, 65, 117
London, England 15, 18, 26, 27, 28, 29, 30, 32, 33, 34, 35, 43, 69, 71, 72, 74, 76, 120, 121, 122
Louisburg Square 72, 74, 76

M

McKim, Charles Follen 12, 17, 18, 35, 36, 47, 52, 54, 55, 84, 85, 86, 87, 89, 90, 91, 95, 96, 97, 98, 99, 106, 109, 110, 118, 119
McKim, Mead & White, Architects 17, 20, 37, 38, 54, 84, 85, 86, 89, 96, 109
Mies van der Rohe, Ludwig 108, 116, 117
Modernism 74, 105, 106, 107, 108, 109, 113, 116, 117, 118, 126
Museum of Fine Arts (Boston) 28, 29, 30, 31, 87
Museum of Modern Art (NYC) 108

138

Index

N

National Historic Landmarks 20, 51
National Trust for Historic Preservation 106
New York City architecture 44, 75, 108, 109

O

Old South Church 20, 31, 37, 39, 67, 71, 103, 104
Orphanage for Children 98, 100
Ospedale degli Innocenti. *See* Orphanage for Children

P

Paris, France 18, 33, 34, 37, 43, 52, 54, 69, 70, 71, 76, 78, 84, 86, 87, 89, 96, 97, 98, 109, 110, 120, 121, 122, 126
parks 79, 80
Pei, I.M. 17, 18, 113, 115, 116, 117, 118, 119
Post-Modernism 108, 109
Pritzker Prize, the 108, 115
Public Garden 19, 25, 44, 71, 76, 78
public transit 11, 21, 44, 105

R

Renaissance 15, 18, 34, 36, 56, 65, 74, 85, 86, 89, 91, 93, 95, 96, 97, 98, 99, 109, 118, 127
Richardson, H.H. 17, 18, 20, 35, 36, 37, 46, 47, 49, 50, 51, 52, 53, 54, 55, 56, 57, 59, 60, 61, 62, 63, 65, 66, 85, 86, 95, 110, 118
Richardsonian Romanesque 50, 51, 55, 59
Romanesque 36, 50, 51, 52, 55, 56, 57, 62, 85, 96, 103, 113, 118, 127
Rome, Italy 18, 33, 34, 36, 37, 43, 56, 85, 89, 94, 96, 97, 98, 99, 120, 122, 125, 127
Roth, Leland M. 90
Ruskin, John 49, 50, 51, 53, 61, 65, 66, 80, 84, 104

S

San Francisco, California 37, 75, 76, 77, 78, 110

T

Trinity Church 17, 18, 20, 25, 36, 38, 39, 41, 46, 47, 49, 50, 51, 52, 53, 54, 55, 57, 59, 60, 61, 62, 63, 64, 65, 66, 71, 72, 85, 86, 95, 103, 104, 108, 110, 113, 115, 116, 117

V

Vatican 98, 99
Venetian color 64
Venetian style 31, 50, 53, 61, 65, 66, 67, 71, 80, 103, 104
Venice, Italy 53, 65, 66, 80, 94, 103

W

Wells Cathedral 62

ABOUT THE AUTHOR

Leslie Humm Cormier, PhD, teaches and writes on the history and theory of art, architecture and urban design in Europe and America. She received her doctorate from Brown University as a Kress Fellow, affording her study in London and Paris. She is the author of a book on the Early Modern era in American architecture, as well as many articles on Modern architecture and urban design in architectural encyclopedias. Previously a faculty member of Harvard University Extension and Radcliffe Seminars, Cormier is currently affiliated with the Boston Architectural College.

Visit us at
www.historypress.com